Editorial

After Lockerbie

There has seldom been such unanimity in the British political class as has come about in the last half of August 2009 with the release of the Libyan prisoner, Abdel Baset Ali al-Megrahi, on compassionate grounds. This was announced by the Scottish Secretary for Justice, Kenny MacAskill, after medical reports forecast that the Libyan was at death's door, having advanced prostate cancer which probably gave him a maximum life expectancy of three months.

Megrahi had been sentenced by three Scottish Judges to life imprisonment, following a highly contentious trial in which the Scottish Courts sat in an American airbase in The Netherlands to hear the case of the Lockerbie bomb. (See below the assessment of Professor Robert Black, who is the first of our chosen witnesses, whose job it was 'to try to ensure that the trial would take place'.) A Pan American passenger jet had been blown up on the 21st December 1988, while flying over the small Scottish town of Lockerbie en route for the United States. The evidence showed that a bomb had been secreted in passenger luggage. It had exploded in mid-air, killing all 259 passengers. A giant fireball fell across the town, killing eleven more people on its way. This was a huge disaster, the largest in British aviation history.

Who could have conceived such an atrocity? The intelligence agencies of the world were not at a loss for an explanation. But they were flummoxed by the problem of how to present what they knew, or indeed, whether to present it.

In a forensic exploration of these dilemmas, Paul Foot published a special number of *Private Eye* called *Lockerbie: The Flight from Justice* (see box). Foot traced the various explanations offered in the press, and carefully followed their mutations as considerations of *realpolitik* influenced the authorities about what stories they felt it appropriate to tell.

The core truth was simple. An Iranian passenger jet carrying pilgrims to Mecca had been shot down by an American warship. Iran Air flight 655 was a commercial flight operated by Iran Air that flew on a Tehran – Bandar Abbas – Dubai route. It was shot down on July 3rd 1988 by the USS *Vincennes* on the Bandar Abbas – Dubai leg. Two hundred and ninety pilgrims perished. There were no survivors.

The USS *Vincennes* was fitted with the Aegis combat system, and it was operating in the Strait of Hormuz under the captaincy of Commander William C. Rogers III. The *Vincennes* was inside Iranian territorial waters, in pursuit of Iranian naval boats, which were supposed to be there.

The American authorities said that the *Vincennes* had mistakenly identified the Iranian plane as an attacking military jet. Since the ship had no business which would entitle it to be in the Strait of Hormuz, this was hardly an excuse for what happened. The Americans fired anti-aircraft missiles, one of which split the plane in two, and damaged its tail and right wing. 'Only afterwards it was realised that the plane had indeed been a civilian airliner.' *Newsweek* came to the conclusion that Captain Rogers was acting 'recklessly and without due care'. The journal also alleged a cover-up by the US Government.

True, the American Government issued notes of regret about the loss of human life, but never admitted any wrongdoing or responsibility. Neither did they apologise. Indeed, they blamed and continued to blame the Iranians for the actions leading to the incident. Fifteen years later, on the 6th November 2003, the International Court of Justice concluded that the American Navy's actions in the Persian Gulf at that time had been unlawful.

Most of the officers involved in the shooting down of the plane were decorated when the ship returned to the United States. President George H. W. Bush awarded Captain Rogers the Legion of Merit decoration, not an ordinary medal, but worn round the neck, for exceptional meritorious conduct in the performance of outstanding service as Commanding Officer from April 1987 to May 1989. The citation did not mention the destruction of Iran Air flight 655.

This is the context in which western journalists and some intelligence agencies came to believe that there was an Iranian influence on the plans to destroy an American passenger flight, or perhaps more than one, by way of reprisal.

It is also the context in which the Iranians evaluated the lack of contrition in the United States about the death of all those pilgrims. Does this not compare with the heartfelt sense of scandal registered by the relatives of the Lockerbie victims in the United States when Abdel al-Megrahi returned to Libya and was afforded what the Western press described as 'a hero's welcome'?

But Megrahi was completely innocent, while Rogers was guilty.

The destruction of the Pan Am jumbo jet in December 1988 was, in other words, generally assumed to be a straightforward act of revenge. All the spooks who spoke, and all the journalists who reported them, homed in on the conclusion that the Popular Front for the Liberation of Palestine General Command, a group based in Syria, had been responsible for the placing of the bomb which brought about the act of vengeance. It was alleged that substantial payments had been made to the PFLP by the Iranian Government.

The Spokesman

Responsibility to Protest

Edited by Ken Coates
Assistant Editor Tony Simpson

Published by Spokesman for the
Bertrand Russell Peace Foundation

Spokesman 105   2009

CONTENTS

Cover: With grateful acknowledgements to Steve Bell

ISSN 1367 7748   Printed by the Russell Press Ltd., Nottingham, UK   ISBN 978 0 85124 772 4

Subscriptions
Institutions £35.00
Individuals £20.00 (UK)
£25.00 (ex UK)

Back issues available
on request

A CIP catalogue record
for this book is available
from the British Library

Published by the
Bertrand Russell Peace
Foundation Ltd.,
Russell House
Bulwell Lane
Nottingham NG6 0BT
England
Tel. 0115 9784504
email:
elfeuro@compuserve.com
www.spokesmanbooks.com
www.russfound.org

FSC
Mixed Sources
Product group from well-managed
forests and other controlled sources

Cert no. SGS-COC-006541
www.fsc.org
© 1996 Forest Stewardship Council

Bertrand Russell
at Routledge

Philosopher, educational and sexual reformer, peace campaigner and prolific letter writer, author and columnist, **Bertrand Russell** was one of the most influential and widely known intellectual figures of the twentieth century. The home of more of his works than any other English language publisher, Routledge will be making its complete Bertrand Russell backlist available in the **Routledge Classics** series in 2009.

All titles NEW in September 2009

£9.99
978-0-415-48733-7

£15.99
978-0-415-47373-6

£9.99
978-0-415-48734-4

£12.99
978-0-415-48735-1

£14.99
978-0-415-48732-0

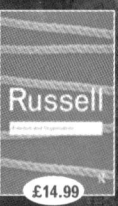
£14.99
978-0-415-48739-9

£12.99
978-0-415-48737-5

£14.99
978-0-415-48740-5

£14.99
978-0-415-48741-2

£12.99
978-0-415-47461-0

£14.99
978-0-415-48736-8

£12.99
978-0-415-48738-2

Routledge Classics: Get Inside A Great Mind

Paul Foot's account of these matters is entirely clear, and he established beyond doubt that the earliest stories about Lockerbie never considered any role for Libyans beyond an apparently peripheral allegation by a Maltese shopkeeper who later figured in the trial.

However, after Saddam Hussein invaded Kuwait, in 1990, international alignments all changed, and Iran and Syria became temporary or potential allies of the United States. Our political classes think that it is a conspiracy theory to say that the shifting of the spotlight from Iran to Libya owes more to diplomatic convenience than to the pursuit of truth. None the less, that happened, and it is not otherwise easy to explain.

Things have since moved on. A growing energy crisis in Europe has now produced a situation in which the European powers perceive the development of an unhealthy dependence upon Russian sources of oil and natural gas. The fact that the Middle East has been visited by cataclysm with the pursuit of various wars on terror has not eased this dependence. Suddenly, Libya becomes a hot property, bubbling with oil and gas, all highly conveniently situated for the supply of energy-famished European

---

Was the bomb loaded at Heathrow?

Paul Foot, in *Lockerbie: The Flight from Justice*, carefully documented the question of which airport the bomb suitcase had started out on its journey to Lockerbie.

> 'As we have seen, there was no evidence that it got on at Malta; and debatable documentation to suggest that it went on at Frankfurt.'

In fact, thought Foot, it was far more likely that it went on at Heathrow. A maroony-brown Samsonite suitcase was noted to be on the baggage container which carried luggage (including the explosive device?) to the plane. This evidence 'came from the man who loaded the container, Heathrow employee John Bedford'.

It was a Samsonite case that exploded with the bomb in it, thirty-eight minutes after take-off from Heathrow. The timers used by the Syrian-based team of saboteurs were designed to explode after thirty-eight minutes. The timers which the Libyans and East German secret police had bought from the Swiss firm MEBO, and which figured in the prosecution's version of events, were different.

In a nutshell, the theory that the bomb had been emplaced in Heathrow, and that it implicated the PFLP team, was far more plausible than the other theories, including that chosen by the prosecution. But the prosecution had got a victim in its sights, and he had the merit of not being an Iranian.

powers. But in the meantime, the Lockerbie trial has taken place, and Mr. Megrahi has been found guilty of bombing Pan Am flight 103.

That is the reason why London politicians, the President of the United States, and the assembled legions of the great and good have all been able to reach accord on the errors of the Scottish justice system, and the wickedness of compassionate release for Mr. al-Megrahi. But evidence does not figure very strongly in this package of gut-reactions. From the first moment, the elaborate Scottish trial conducted in The Netherlands has provoked severe misgivings.

We feature below the report by Dr. Hans Köchler, the international observer appointed by Kofi Annan to cover the trial. He placed on record his 'suspicion that political considerations may have been overriding a strictly judicial evaluation of the case, and thus may have adversely affected the outcome of the trial'. More: the trial 'may to a considerable extent have been the result of more or less openly exercised influence from the part of actors outside the judicial framework'.

On the basis of his observation of the trial and careful scrutiny of its procedures, the UN observer 'reached the conclusion that the trial, seen in its entirety, was not fair and was not conducted in an objective manner'.

None of the British political lions have paid any attention to the UN Rapporteur. But neither have they been influenced unduly by the Scottish Criminal Cases Review Commission, which determined that Megrahi was entitled to a further appeal against his conviction. This judgment extends to eight-hundred-plus pages, and is accompanied by thirteen further volumes of appendices. Amongst other things, the Commission wanted to know whether the key prosecution witnesses might have been swayed by the prospect of a $2 million reward proposed by the Scottish police to the American authorities. The Scottish police also generously suggested that the witness's brother, who had provided corroboration, should be paid an additional $1 million. Initially, two Libyans had been charged, but one had been acquitted because it was established that the witness of his alleged misdemeanours had already been paid $4 million for his testimony. The Criminal Cases Review Commission named six grounds which could indicate a serious miscarriage of justice in the Megrahi case, and yet almost every newspaper has pretended that the guilt of Mr. Megrahi is established beyond any reasonable doubt. So have all those pious and loyal politicians. *The Mail on Sunday*, however, published in its Scottish edition Tam Dalyell's heretical interpretation of events, which we also reprint below.

True, there are limiting influences which can mitigate the hysteria unleashed against the Scottish Government and its spokesmen. Not the least of these is the fact that Mr. Blair had indeed cut a series of deals with President Gadaffi which provided important inducements to the British Government not to undo their relationships with the Libyan leader. (See box – Doing business in Libya.)

The fish rots from the head

Tony Blair made two visits to Libya, where, on each occasion, he met with President Gadaffi. The ice was broken in 2004, and in May 2007 Tripoli agreed to buy British missiles and air defence systems from British Aerospace in a very large deal. The Libyans also agreed on a gas exploration deal worth 'at least $900 million' (£509 million). Of course, big deals have been going on all the time. Mr. Blair is himself quite a large operator, having been paid $5 million a year for his work for the investment bank J. P. Morgan. This works out at £3 million at the current exchange rate. BP, which engaged Blair's former assistant, Angie Hunter, as an adviser to Lord Browne, and liaison with the premier, 'helped to earn the company the damaging sobriquet "Blair Petroleum",' was among a number of British companies which ended a thirty year absence from Libya in 2007 with a bilateral exploration commitment to drill in the onshore Ghadames area and also in the offshore Sirte Basin, with seventeen exploratory wells.

Doing business in Libya

'Britain will be hoping for smoother business ties with Libya after the release of convicted Lockerbie bomber Abdel Basset al-Megrahi. The North African country was off-limits for decades and British and other oil firms agreed tough terms when they were at last able to sign exploration and production deals there.

Following is a list of some of the biggest foreign oil companies in Libya. Information is taken from previous Reuters stories.

BP – The British firm ended a 30-year absence from Libya in 2007 when it signed its biggest ever exploration commitment through a bilateral deal. It will spend at least $900 million to search the onshore Ghadames area and offshore Sirte Basin with 17 exploration wells.

Royal Dutch Shell – the London-listed company was awarded a gas exploration permit in 2007 for areas in the Sirte Basin, and was also awarded permits in 2005.

ExxonMobil – in February 2008 the US oil major agreed with Libya's national oil company to invest $97 million plus tens of millions in fees in offshore hydrocarbon exploration. The company in 2005 struck an exploration and production sharing deal with Libya's state oil company

---

that covers the Cyrenaica Basin, covering 2.5 million acres, from deep to shallow waters.

Verenex – The Canadian company is the only winner of post-sanctions licences under Libya's EPSA-IV tender mechanism to have made sizeable finds, prompting a battle for ownership of the company between Libya and China National Petroleum Corp.

Occidental – The company which began business in Libya in 1966, reported first-quarter 2009 net production from Libya of 8,000 barrels per day, down from 22,000 bpd a year earlier. In late 2007 it won gas-focused permits to explore areas of the Sirte Basin, and in 2005 was the biggest winner in Libya's first licensing round.

PGNiG – Libya's state-owned oil corporation ratified a gas exploration agreement in February 2008 with the Polish gas monopoly for drilling at least eight wells at a cost of $108 million in the Murzuq Basin.

Gazprom – The Russian company was awarded a gas exploration licence in 2007 for areas in the Ghadames Basin.

RWE – The German energy firm agreed to spend at least $76 million and drill two exploration wells in Syrenica Basin blocks it won access to in late 2007.

Sonatrach – The Algerian state energy firm won blocks in the Ghadames Basin in December 2007.

Oasis Group – in December 2005 the consortium of ConocoPhillips, Amerada Hess and Marathon agreed to pay Libya $1.3 billion to extend their contracts in the Sirte Basin. The contracts were concluded before the sanctions were imposed, but the US companies left Libya in 1986 after US sanctions were imposed.

Nippon Oil – Japan's largest refiner in 2005 struck an offshore exploration and production sharing agreement with Libya that also includes Mitsubishi Corp. and Japan Petroleum Exploration (JAPEX), which said it would invest $48 million in exploration over five years.

Petrobas – The Brazilian company was awarded licences for exploring offshore in January 2005.

Following are some other companies with business ties with Libya, according to the British-Libyan Business Council:

BNP Paribas – Bought a 19 per cent stake and strategic partnership in Sahara Bank for 145 million in 2007, the first partial privatisation deal for Libya.

Barclays, HSBC, Standard Chartered, J. P. Morgan Asset Management.'

Source: Aug 20 2009, 9.35 a.m. Eastern Daylight Time from Reuters on Bester News.

Lockerbie and the Law

Robert Black

The author is Professor of Scots Law at the University of Edinburgh. He was one of the architects of the trial of the two Libyans at Camp Zeist. Here he gives his views on the original investigation, Megrahi's trial, his appeal, and the impact of the case on the Scottish justice system. This article was originally published in the Scottish newspaper The Herald *on 21 August 2009.*

The Investigation

Within a week of the tragedy the joint team of British and American investigators had formed the view that this had been no accident and that the cause of the destruction of the aircraft had been a bomb. There then followed the most extensive criminal investigation ever conducted in Scotland – or, it seems probably, anywhere else – into an act of terrorism.

It came as something of a surprise when on November 14th 1991, the prosecution authorities in Scotland and the US simultaneously announced that they had brought criminal charges against two named Libyan nationals who were alleged to be members, and to have been acting throughout as agents, of the Libyan intelligence service.

Until then all of the leaks were that the atrocity had been committed by Ahmed Jibril's Syrian-backed Popular Front for the Liberation of Palestine-General Command.

Until the trial actually started I had no idea what the evidence was going to be and had no idea what the outcome was going to be. My job was to try to ensure that the trial would take place. It was what I heard at the trial that then gave rise to grave concerns.

The Trial at Camp Zeist

The prosecution in their closing submissions conceded that the case against the accused was entirely circumstantial. That, of course, is no bar to a verdict of guilty. But to many observers, including me, it seemed that the case presented by the prosecution was a very weak circumstantial one, and was further undermined by the additional prosecution concession that they had not been able to prove how the bomb that destroyed Pan Am 103 got into the interline baggage system and on to the aircraft.

Before the verdicts in the original trial were delivered, I expressed the view that for the judges to return verdicts of guilty they would require:

(i)   to accept every incriminating inference that the Crown invited them to draw from evidence that was on the face of it neutral and capable of supporting quite innocent inferences,

(ii) to be satisfied beyond reasonable doubt that the Maltese shopkeeper, Tony Gauci, positively identified Megrahi as the person who bought from his shop in Sliema the clothes and umbrella contained in the suitcase that held the bomb, and

(iii) to accept that the date of purchase of these items was proved to be December 7th 1988 (as distinct from November 23rd 1988 when Megrahi was not present on Malta).

I went on rashly to express the opinion that, for the judges to be satisfied of all these matters on the evidence led at the trial, they would require to adopt the posture of the White Queen in *Through the Looking-Glass*, when she informed Alice: 'Why, sometimes I've believed as many as six impossible things before breakfast'. In convicting Megrahi, it is submitted that this is precisely what the trial judges did.

I am absolutely convinced that if the evidence had come out in front of a Scottish jury of fifteen there is absolutely no way he would have been convicted.

The judges didn't appear to give themselves the instructions that they always give to a jury – the perfectly bog standard instructions that every jury in every Scottish criminal trial gets about how to approach the evidence.

The Appeals Process

As far as the outcome of the first appeal is concerned, some commentators have confidently opined that, in dismissing Megrahi's appeal, the Appeal Court endorsed the findings of the trial court. This is not so. The Appeal Court repeatedly stresses that it is not its function to approve or disapprove of the trial court's findings-in-fact, given that it was not contended on behalf of the appellant that there was insufficient evidence to warrant them, or that no reasonable court could have made them. These findings-in-fact accordingly continue, as before the appeal, to have the authority only of the court which, and the three judges who, made them.

I had hoped that the appeal court in the second appeal would have addressed the fundamental issues of:

(i) whether there was sufficient evidence to warrant the incriminating findings,

(ii) whether any reasonable trial court could have made those findings (and could have been satisfied beyond reasonable doubt of the guilt of Megrahi) on the evidence led at Camp Zeist and

(iii) whether Megrahi's representation at the trial and the appeal was adequate.

This will not happen, because Mr. Megrahi sadly felt he had to abandon his second appeal, and I will continue to maintain that a shameful miscarriage of justice has been perpetrated and that the Scottish criminal justice system has been gravely sullied.

Kenny MacAskill's Role

I have a great deal of sympathy with him. I am sorry he had to take so long to reach the decision. However, in some respects it is just as well he did. He actually rejected the prisoner transfer application. If Megrahi hadn't belatedly put in an application for compassionate release he would still be in prison today. Perhaps the delay did serve a useful purpose. As Kenny correctly said in making his decision, he has to assume that Megrahi was properly convicted.

Impact of the Case

If the approach is that everybody simply says, 'He abandoned his appeal and has been released on compassionate grounds, everything is therefore for the best', then it is a very sad day for the Scottish criminal justice system because no lessons have been learned.

My God, lessons need to be learned out of Lockerbie.

We have relied too much on those professionals in the system knowing what is the right thing to do and doing it almost instinctively. I am afraid that is simply no longer good enough.

There is still a cloud hanging over Megrahi's conviction. Until that cloud is removed then the criminal justice system cannot legitimately claim to be one of the best in the world.

Unfair Trial

Hans Köchler

A report by Dr Köchler on the Lockerbie Trial conducted by the special Scottish Court in The Netherlands at Kamp van Zeist. Dr Köchler, university professor and member of the International Progress Organization, was nominated as observer at the trial by United Nations Secretary-General Kofi Annan on the basis of Security Council resolution 1192 (1998).

The undersigned observed the proceedings of the High Court of Justiciary at Camp Zeist (Netherlands) since the beginning on 5 May 2000 until the announcement of the verdict and sentence in the causa Her Majesty's Advocate v Abdelbasset Ali Mohamed Al Megrahi and Al Amin Khalifa Fhimah on 31 January 2001. He regularly attended the sessions of the Court, repeatedly met with the prosecution and defence teams, interviewed the Registrar and staff members of the Scottish Court Service at Kamp van Zeist, inspected HM Prison Zeist, met with the Governor and Deputy Governor of HM Prison Zeist and with the Chief of the Scottish Police at Kamp van Zeist. He interviewed the two accused Libyan nationals at the beginning of the trial and again – in separate meetings – after the passing of the verdict and sentence on 31 January 2001. All meetings were arranged through the Scottish Court Service. The undersigned further had access to the complete transcripts of the Court's proceedings and exchanged notes with the additional international observer of the International Progress Organization, Mr. Robert Thabit, Esq.

On the basis of his first exploratory visit to Kamp van Zeist and of the interview with the two accused, the undersigned, in May 2000, sent a confidential message to the Secretary-General of the United Nations. He made no public comments during the entire period of the trial and did not seek a meeting with the panel of judges, Lord Sutherland, Lord Coulsfield and Lord Maclean. He exercised his observer mission on the basis of respect of the constitutional independence of the judiciary and *interpreted his mission – in the absence of any specific description of the tasks of international observers in the respective Security Council resolution – in the sense of evaluating the aspects of due process and fairness of the trial. He reached agreement on the nature of this observer mission with the additional observer of the International Progress Organization, Mr. Robert Thabit.*

* * *

Based on his observations during the entire period of the trial and on the information obtained in the numerous meetings with the protagonists of the trial mentioned above, the undersigned presents the following evaluation in regard to the aspect of due process and the question of the fairness of the trial:

1. All administrative aspects of the trial were handled with great care, efficiency and professionalism by the staff of the Scottish Court Service at Kamp van Zeist. Apart from minor problems with simultaneous interpretation at the beginning of the trial, there were no major weaknesses that might have affected the fairness of the proceedings. The problems of interpretation were solved in a satisfactory manner. The Scottish Court Service did its best to assist the undersigned in the accomplishment of his observer mission.

2. The circumstances of detention of the two accused at Her Majesty's Prison Zeist were in conformity with national legal requirements and international legal and human rights standards. According to the information given by the accused in a private interview with the undersigned, no people had access to them without their consent. In particular, the medical services and the medical care for the second accused (who needs permanent medication) were up to the required standard. Upon their special request, the undersigned sent a note about his meeting with the accused in May 2000 and conveyed their concerns in regard to certain political aspects of the United Nations arrangements and conditions for their coming to the Netherlands to the Secretary-General of the United Nations. The Governor of HM Prison Zeist forwarded the undersigned's confirmation note on the forwarding of this message to the two accused. The prison administration was fully co-operative in regard to the undersigned's requests in the exercise of his observer mission.

3. The extraordinary length of detention of the two suspects/accused from the time of their arrival in The Netherlands until the beginning of the trial in May 2000 has constituted a serious problem in regard to the basic human rights of the two Libyan nationals under general European

standards, in particular those of the European Convention on Human Rights. In general, the highly political circumstances of the trial and special security considerations related to the political nature of the trial may have had a detrimental effect on the rights of the accused, in particular in regard to the duration of administrative detention.

4. As far as the material aspects of due process and fairness of the trial are concerned, the presence of at least two representatives of a foreign government in the courtroom during the entire period of the trial was highly problematic. The two state prosecutors from the US Department of Justice were seated next to the prosecution team. They were not listed in any of the official information documents about the Court's officers produced by the Scottish Court Service, yet they were seen talking to the prosecutors while the Court was in session, checking notes and passing on documents. For an independent observer watching this from the visitors' gallery, this created the impression of 'supervisors' handling vital matters of the prosecution strategy and deciding, in certain cases, which documents (evidence) were to be released in open court or what parts of information contained in a certain document were to be withheld (deleted).

5. This serious problem of due process became evident in the matter of the CIA cables concerning one of the Crown's key witnesses, Mr. Giaka. Those cables were initially dismissed by the prosecution as 'not relevant', but proved to be of high relevance when finally (though only partially) released after a move from the part of the defence. Apart from this specific aspect – that seriously damaged the integrity of the whole legal procedure – it has become obvious that the presence of representatives of foreign governments in a Scottish courtroom (or any courtroom, for that matter) on the side of the prosecution team jeopardizes the independence and integrity of legal procedures and is not in conformity with the general standards of due process and fairness of the trial. As has become obvious to the undersigned, this presence has negatively impacted on the Court's ability to find the truth; it has introduced a political element into the proceedings in the courtroom. This presence should never have been granted from the outset.

6. Another, though less serious, problem in regard to due process was the presence of foreign nationals on the side of the defence team in the courtroom during the whole period of the trial. Apart from the presence of an Arab interpreter (which was perfectly reasonable under aspects of fairness and efficiency of the proceedings), the presence of a Libyan lawyer who had held high posts in the Libyan government and who represented the Libyan Jamahiriya in its case v the United States and the United Kingdom at the International Court of Justice gave the trial a

political aspect that should have been avoided by decision of the panel of judges. Though Mr. Maghour acted officially as Libyan defence lawyer for the accused Libyan nationals and although he was not seen by the undersigned as interacting with the Scottish defence lawyers during court proceedings, he had to be perceived as a kind of liaison official in a political sense. It has to be noted that the original Libyan defence lawyer, Dr. Ibrahim Legwell (chosen by the two suspects long before their transfer to The Netherlands), resigned under protest when the Libyan government introduced Mr. Maghour as new defence lawyer for the two accused. In sum, the presence of *de facto* governmental representatives of both sides in the courtroom gave the trial a highly political aura that should have been avoided by all means, at least as far as the actual proceedings in the courtroom were concerned. Again, as to the undersigned's knowledge, the presence of foreign nationals on the side of the defence team was mentioned in no official briefing document of the Scottish Court Service.

7. It was a consistent pattern during the whole trial that – as an apparent result of political interests and considerations – efforts were undertaken to withhold substantial information from the Court. One of the most obvious cases in point was that of the former Libyan double agent, Abdul Majid Giaka, and the CIA cables related to him. Some of the cables were finally released after much insistence from the part of the defence, some were never made available. The Court was apparently content with this situation, which is hard to understand for an independent observer. It may never be fully known up to which extent relevant information was hidden from the Court. The most serious case, however, is related to the special defence launched by defence attorneys Taylor and Keen. It was officially stated by the Lord Advocate that substantial new information had been received from an unnamed foreign government relating to the defence case. The content of this information was never revealed, the requested specific documents were never provided by a foreign government. The alternative theory of the defence – leading to conclusions contradictory to those of the prosecution – was never seriously investigated. Amid shrouds of secrecy and 'national security' considerations, that avenue was never seriously pursued – although it was officially declared as being of major importance for the defence case. This is totally incomprehensible to any rational observer. By not having pursued thoroughly and carefully an alternative theory, the Court seems to have accepted that the whole legal process was seriously flawed in regard to the requirements of objectivity and due process.

8. As a result of this situation, the undersigned has reached the

conclusion that foreign governments or (secret) governmental agencies may have been allowed, albeit indirectly, to determine, to a considerable extent, which evidence was made available to the Court.

9. In the analysis of the undersigned, the strategy of the defence team by suddenly dropping its 'special defence' and cancelling the appearance of almost all defence witnesses (in spite of the defence's ambitious announcements made earlier during the trial) is totally incomprehensible; it puts into question the credibility of the defence's actions and motives. In spite of repeated requests of the undersigned, the defence lawyers were not available for comment on this particular matter.

10. A general pattern of the trial consisted in the fact that virtually all people presented by the prosecution as key witnesses were proven to lack credibility to a very high extent, in certain cases even having openly lied to the Court. Particularly as regards Mr. Bollier and Mr. Giaka, there were so many inconsistencies in their statements and open contradictions to statements of other witnesses that the resulting confusion was much greater than any clarification that may have been obtained from parts of their statements. Their credibility as such was shaken. It seems highly arbitrary and irrational to choose only parts of their statements for the formulation of a verdict that requires certainty 'beyond any reasonable doubt'.

11. The air of international power politics is present in the whole verdict of the panel of judges. In spite of the many reservations in the Opinion of the Court explaining the verdict itself, the guilty verdict in the case of the first accused is particularly incomprehensible in view of the admission by the judges themselves that the identification of the first accused by the Maltese shop owner was 'not absolute' (formulation in Par. 89 of the Opinion) and that there was a 'mass of conflicting evidence' (*ibid.*). The consistency and legal credibility of the verdict is further jeopardized by the fact that the judges deleted one of the basic elements of the indictment, namely the statement about the two accused having induced on 20 December 1988 into Malta airport the suitcase that was supposedly used to hide the bomb that exploded in the Pan Am jet.

12. Furthermore, the Opinion of the Court seems to be inconsistent in a basic respect: while the first accused was found 'guilty', the second accused was found 'not guilty'. It is to be noted that the judgment, in the latter's case, was *not* 'not proven', but 'not guilty'. This is totally incomprehensible for any rational observer when one considers that the indictment in its very essence was based on the joint action of the two accused in Malta.

13. The Opinion of the Court is exclusively based on circumstantial

evidence and on a series of highly problematic inferences. As to the undersigned's knowledge, there is not one single piece of material evidence linking the two accused to the crime. In such a context, the guilty verdict in regard to the first accused appears to be arbitrary, even irrational. This impression is enforced when one considers that the actual wording of the larger part of the Opinion of the Court points more into the direction of a 'not proven' verdict. The arbitrary aspect of the verdict is becoming even more obvious when one considers that the prosecution, at a rather late stage of the trial, decided to 'split' the accusation and to change the very essence of the indictment by renouncing the identification of the second accused as a member of Libyan intelligence so as to actually disengage him from the formerly alleged collusion with the first accused in the supposed perpetration of the crime. Some light is shed on this procedure by the otherwise totally incomprehensible 'not guilty' verdict in regard to the second accused.

14. This leads the undersigned to the suspicion that political considerations may have been overriding a strictly judicial evaluation of the case and thus may have adversely affected the outcome of the trial. This may have a profound impact on the evaluation of the professional reputation and integrity of the panel of three Scottish judges. Seen from the final outcome, a certain coordination of the strategies of the prosecution, of the defence, and of the judges' considerations during the later period of the trial is not totally unlikely. This, however, – when actually proven – would have a devastating effect on the whole legal process of the Scottish Court in the Netherlands and on the legal quality of its findings.

15. In the above context, the undersigned has reached the general conclusion that the outcome of the trial may well have been determined by political considerations and may to a considerable extent have been the result of more or less openly exercised influence from the part of actors outside the judicial framework – facts which are not compatible with the basic principle of the division of powers and with the independence of the judiciary, and which put in jeopardy the very rule of law and the confidence citizens must have in the legitimacy of state power and the functioning of the state's organs – whether on the traditional national level or in the framework of international justice as it is gradually being established through the United Nations Organization.

16. On the basis of the above observations and evaluation, the undersigned has – to his great dismay – reached the conclusion that the trial, seen in its entirety, was not fair and was not conducted in an objective manner. Indeed, there are many more questions and doubts at the end of

the trial than there were at its beginning. The trial has effectively created more confusion than clarity and no rational observer can make any statement on the complex subject matter 'beyond any reasonable doubt'. Irrespective of this regrettable outcome, the search for the truth must continue. This is the requirement of the rule of law and the right of the victims' families and of the international public.

17. The international observer may draw one general conclusion from the conduct of the trial, which allows to formulate a general maxim applicable to judicial procedures in general: proper judicial procedure is simply impossible if political interests and intelligence services – from whichever side – succeed in interfering in the actual conduct of a court. We should remember the wisdom of Immanuel Kant who – in his treatise on perpetual peace (*Zum ewigen Frieden*), elaborating on the essence of the rule of law – unambiguously stated that secrecy is never compatible with a republican system determined by the rule of law. The purpose of intelligence services – from whichever side – lies in secret action and deception, not in the search for truth. Justice and the rule of law can never be achieved without transparency.

18. Regrettably, through the conduct of the Court, disservice has been done to the important cause of international criminal justice. The goals of criminal justice on an international level cannot be advanced in a context of power politics and in the absence of an elaborate division of powers. What is true on the national level, applies to the transnational level as well. No national court can function if it has to act under pressure from the executive power and if vital evidence is being withheld from it because of political interests. The realities faced by the Scottish Court in The Netherlands have demonstrated this truth in a very clear and dramatic fashion – the political impact stemming, in this particular case, from a highly complex web of national and transnational interests related to the interaction among several major actors on the international scene.

19. The undersigned would like to express his humble opinion – or hope, for that matter – that an appeal, if granted, will correct the deficiencies of the trial as explained above. It goes without saying that all will depend on the integrity and independence of the five judges of an eventual Court of Appeal operating under Scottish law.

20. The above evaluation should in no way be interpreted as to diminish the idealistic contribution and commitment of so many civil servants of the Scottish Court Service and the Scottish police authorities who guaranteed the smooth functioning of the whole court operation at Kamp van Zeist under difficult and truly extraordinary circumstances.

The undersigned would like to emphasize that the above remarks constitute a personal evaluation by himself alone and that he is only bound by the dictates of his conscience; as an international citizen committed to the goals and principles of the United Nations Charter, he does not accept any pressure or influence from the part of any government, political party or interest group.

Truth in a matter of criminal justice has to be found through a transparent inquiry that will only be possible if all considerations of power politics are put aside. The rule of law is not compatible with the rules of power politics; justice cannot be done unless in complete independence, based on reason and the unequivocal commitment to basic human rights.

Dr. Hans Köchler

From *The Times*
September 4, 2009

Al-Megrahi: a miscarriage of justice
Why al-Megrahi should not have abandoned his appeal

Sir, I was a member of the team of lawyers who acted for Abdul Baset Ali al-Megrahi in his claim against the UK of breach of the right to a fair trial under the European Human Rights Convention. I met him in prison and, after carefully studying the transcripts of his trial and the judgments of the Scottish courts, came to the conclusion that he had been the victim of a serious miscarriage of justice.

The European Court of Human Rights rejected his claim without even communicating it to the Government, but the Scottish Criminal Cases Review Commission was sufficiently concerned to refer the case back to the Scottish judiciary.

I express no opinion about the decision to allow Mr al-Megrahi to return to die in Libya. But in my view, it is a misfortune that he has been induced to abandon his appeal. Had the appeal proceeded, it would have given him the opportunity to clear his name not only for his sake but also for the sake of the families bereaved by the mass murder at Lockerbie.

Lord Lester of Herne Hill, QC
House of Lords

Lockerbie –
The Cover-up

Marcello Mega

The author is a free-lance journalist. We are grateful to him and to the Mail on Sunday *(Scottish edition) for permission to reprint this article which was originally published on 16 August 2009.*

The wrong man was jailed for the Lockerbie bombing and the real suspect allowed to escape justice to satisfy political motives, a damning investigation can reveal.

The Scottish Mail on Sunday can today publish remarkable details from a report by two leading investigators which throws major doubt on the conviction of Libyan agent Abdel-baset Ali Mohmed Al Megrahi. He is expected to be freed from a Scottish prison this week after serving eight years of a life sentence for the bombing. The report would have formed the basis of Megrahi's appeal against his conviction, a case which will never be heard after he dropped his legal challenge in return for his early release.

The investigation finds that the man almost certain to have conducted the attack was Mohammed Abu Talb, a convicted Palestinian terrorist with the backing, finance, equipment and contacts to have carried out the atrocity. It also places Talb at the scene where parts of the suitcase bomb were bought – and in Britain when it exploded over Lockerbie. But instead of pursuing Talb and his Iranian backers, the report claims the American and British manhunt was ordered to find a link to Libya and its leader, Colonel Gaddafi.

In a damning verdict on the case, the investigators conclude:

'We are convinced Mr ... Megrahi's conviction was based on flawed evidence ... Megrahi's conviction was based on fundamentally flawed evidence. We have never seen a criminal investigation in which there has been such a persistent disregard of an alternative and far more persuasive theory of the case. This leads us to believe the investigation into the Lockerbie bombing was directed off-course as a result of government interference.'

Talb, serving a life sentence in Sweden for a fatal bombing campaign in the Eighties, was a key witness in the prosecution case against Megrahi in the Scottish courts, for which he received immunity from prosecution. However, the investigation on behalf of Megrahi's defence team by a former UK terror chief and a former US prosecutor who has worked for the British government provides compelling evidence that Talb was the bomber. The report reveals that:

● Talb had clothing from the same Maltese shop as that packed in the suitcase that carried the bomb on board Pan Am Flight 103;
● Talb's alibi that he was in Sweden at the time of the bombing was false, he was in London meeting other terrorists with an unprimed bomb;
● Talb had bribed a corrupt employee at Heathrow to get a suit case through security unchecked;
● Talb was paid $500,000 only four months after the bombing.

Megrahi is expected to fly to Libya after being granted his freedom on compassionate grounds. Officials insist the move followed assurances he has terminal cancer and has only three months to live. However, it is also understood that a condition of Megrahi's release was that he dropped his appeal, because the UK Government and the Scottish justice system were keen to prevent embarrassing details about the case emerging.

At the centre of the alleged cover-up is evidence that Libya, then a pariah state to the US and Britain, was singled out for responsibility to suit political motives, when in fact the bombing was carried out by Talb on the orders and funding of Iran in revenge for the shooting down of its airliner by a US warship.

The *Scottish Mail on Sunday* has uncovered much of the evidence that would be a source of embarrassment. In recent years, we have revealed that critical evidence was manipulated and even planted, that the key witness was coached by detectives and rewarded for his ever-changing statements and that recent forensic tests conducted on crucial items of evidence shattered the Crown's case.

Now we have obtained documents which outline evidence that the leading player responsible for taking 270 lives in Lockerbie on December 21, 1988, was not Megrahi but Talb. The report carries weight because of the calibre of those who amassed the evidence - Jessica de Grazia, a former senior New York prosecutor who led an investigation for the UK Attorney General's office into the Serious Fraud Office, and Philip Corbett, a former deputy head of Scotland Yard's Anti-Terrorist Branch. Their access to informed sources in Middle East intelligence gives their report particular authority.

Instructed by Megrahi's defence team after his conviction in January

2001, de Grazia and Corbett placed Talb in key locations in Europe with terrorist leaders in the months prior to the Lockerbie bombing. Much of the evidence implicating Talb was known to the Crown and defence prior to the trial of Megrahi. Talb had links to at least two terror groups, in particular the Popular Front for the Liberation of Palestine - General Command (PFLP-GC) and was a strong suspect. The PFLP-GC, funded by Iran and led by the Syrian Ahmed Jibril, was the first suspect in the Lockerbie case. A cell based in Europe in 1988 was led by Jibril's deputy, Hafez Dalkamoni, with Talb one of their most trusted lieutenants.

However, despite the belief that Iran was responsible, the outbreak of the first Gulf War in 1990 caused a major political shift in the investigation. A secret deal for Allied war-planes to use Iranian airspace to attack Iraq required the US and British governments to stop its pursuit of the Lockerbie bombers and their Iranian connections. Libya was instead chosen as the prime suspect.

When the focus of the investigation switched, the evidence gathered against Talb and the PFLP-GC was effectively discarded by Scottish and US investigators. However, de Grazia and Corbett say evidence almost certainly proved an Iranian-backed plot.

Five months before Lockerbie, the American vessel USS *Vincennes* shot down an Iranian Airbus over the Persian Gulf. All 290 people on board perished. Iran vowed vengeance and promised that the skies would run with the blood of Americans. Three months later, in October 1988, German secret police raided a flat in Germany where Dalkamoni's cell was making Semtex bombs contained in Toshiba radio-cassettes designed to bring down aircraft, identical to the device used in the Lockerbie attack two months later. Although the Germans seized five devices, the bombmaker Marwan Khreesat told them a sixth had been removed by Dalkamoni.

De Grazia and Corbett's investigation reveals that Dalkamoni and Talb had been friends since 1980 and met, including in Malta, in the weeks before the bombing. De Grazia was also told by intelligence sources that 'because of his abilities, Talb was given Lockerbie to carry out'. The investigation says the missing bomb from Germany was probably taken to Malta for safe-keeping before being packed, unprimed, by Talb before its journey to London.

A Maltese connection had also been a focal point of the prosecution's case during Megrahi's trial. They argued that shopkeeper Tony Gauci identified Megrahi as the buyer of clothes later packed in the bomb case. However, de Grazia and Corbett say that Gauci also identified Talb as the man who 'most resembled' the buyer. Although Gauci's evidence about

Megrahi provided key eyewitness evidence to the prosecution's case, it emerged that the store owner had been given paid holidays to Scotland as well as being coached by investigators in his evidence. De Grazia and Corbett say Gauci's evidence against Talb would have been just as strong if it had been pursued. Their report says the most conclusive link between Talb and the clothing bought from Gauci's shop was the discovery of a cardigan in his flat in Sweden. The cardigan was traced to a manufacturer on the Maltese island of Gozo, a firm that supplied Gauci.

The investigation says, based on their evidence, the plan was to launch the attack from Malta but this was dropped because of security at the island's airport. Talb and his colleagues decided Heathrow's security would be easier to crack. It emerged after the bombing there had been a security breach at Heathrow when a lock was forced near Pan Am's airside berths. Corbett describes the probe into the breach as 'inadequate'. Their inquiries uncovered evidence that on an earlier visit to London, Talb bribed an employee to get an unchecked case airside.

Crucially, the report exposes Talb's alibi for December 21. He was not, as he claimed, caring for the children of a relative who was giving birth in a Swedish hospital. They found that on December 19 he sailed from Sweden to Britain, arriving in London on December 21, the day of the bombing. There he met other terrorists, including bomber Abu Elias and Martin Imandi, who are thought to have been in possession of the device left on Flight 103.

After the bombing, De Grazia and Corbett say more evidence emerges linking Talb and his terror cell to the atrocity. They highlight evidence obtained via ex-CIA agent Robert Baer that the Iranian government paid $11 million into a European bank account held by the PFLP-GC two days later. An account held by Talb in Frankfurt was later credited with $500,000.

In their conclusions, De Grazia and Corbett recommend forensic scrutiny of the timer fragment that was the only physical evidence in the case that pointed to Libya. That work showed the fragment had never been near an explosion, shattering the case against Mcgrahi.

The evidence gathered by De Grazia and Corbett would have been the cornerstone of Megrahi's appeal which was expected to have posed a serious challenge to his conviction. However, on Tuesday, as part of the private understanding between the dying Megrahi and the Scottish Executive, his lawyers will drop his appeal. The move will effectively close the chapter on Lockerbie, denying the public the opportunity to hear the full story behind the horror of December 21,1988.

The crime of Lockerbie

Tam Dalyell

Tam Dalyell was MP for Linlithgow for 43 years and Father of the House of Commons when he retired from Westminster in 2005. This article was originally published in the Scottish edition of The Mail on Sunday *on 16 August 2009 and is reprinted with grateful acknowledgements.*

Why have US Secretary of State Hillary Clinton and her officials responded to the return of Megrahi with such a volcanic reaction? The answer is straightforward. The last thing that Washington wants is the truth to emerge about the role of the US in the crime of Lockerbie. I understand the grief of those parents, such as Kathleen Flynn and Bert Ammerman, who have appeared on our TV screens to speak about the loss of loved ones. Alas all these years they have been lied to about the cause of that grief.

Not only did Washington not want the awful truth to emerge, but Mrs Thatcher, a few – very few – in the stratosphere of Whitehall and certain officials of the Crown Office in Edinburgh, who owe their subsequent careers to the Lockerbie investigation, were compliant.

It all started in July 1988 with the shooting down by the warship USS *Vincennes* of an Iranian airliner carrying 290 pilgrims to Mecca – without an apology. The Iranian minister of the interior at the time was Ali Akbar Mostashemi, who made a public statement that blood would rain down in the form of ten western airliners being blown out of the sky.

Mostashemi was in a position to carry out such a threat – he had been the Iranian ambassador in Damascus from 1982 to 1984 and had developed close relations with the terrorist gangs of Beirut and the Bekaa Valley – and in particular terrorist leader Abu Nidal and Ahmed Jibril, the head of the Popular Front for the Liberation of Palestine – General Command.

Washington was appalled. I believe so appalled and fearful that it entered into a

Faustian agreement that, tit-for-tat, one airliner should be sacrificed. This may seem a dreadful thing for me to say. But consider the facts. A notice went up in the US Embassy in Moscow advising diplomats not to travel with Pan Am back to America for Christmas. American military personnel were pulled off the plane. A delegation of South Africans, including foreign minister Pik Botha, were pulled off Pan Am Flight 103 at the last minute.

Places became available. Who took them at the last minute? The students. Jim Swire's daughter, John Mosey's daughter, Martin Cadman's son, Pamela Dix's brother, other British relatives, many of whom you have seen on television in recent days, and, crucially, 32 students of the University of Syracuse, New York.

If it had become known – it was the interregnum between Ronald Reagan demitting office and George Bush Snr entering the White House – that, in the light of the warning, Washington had pulled VIPs but had allowed Bengt Carlsson, the UN negotiator for Angola whom it didn't like, and the youngsters to travel to their deaths, there would have been an outcry of US public opinion. No wonder the government of the United States and key officials do not want the world to know what they have done.

If you think that this is fanciful, consider more facts. When the relatives went to see the then UK Transport Secretary, Cecil Parkinson, he told them he did agree that there should be a public inquiry. Going out of the door as they were leaving, as an afterthought he said: 'Just one thing. I must clear permission for a public inquiry with colleagues'. Dr Swire, John Mosey and Pamela Dix, the secretary of the Lockerbie relatives, imagined that it was a mere formality. A fortnight later, sheepishly, Parkinson informed them that colleagues had not agreed. At that time there was only one colleague who could possibly have told Parkinson that he was forbidden to do something in his own department. That was the Prime Minister. Only she could have told Parkinson to withdraw his offer, certainly, in my opinion, knowing the man, given in good faith.

Fast forward 13 years. I was the chairman of the all-party House of Commons group on Latin America. I had hosted Dr Alvaro Uribe, the President of Colombia, between the time that he won the election and formally took control in Bogota. The Colombian Ambassador, Victor Ricardo, invited me to dinner at his residence as Dr Uribe wanted to continue the conversations with me.

The South Americans are very formal. A man takes a woman in to dinner. To make up numbers, Ricardo had invited a little old lady, his neighbour. I was mandated to take her in to dinner. The lady was Margaret Thatcher, to whom I hadn't spoken for 17 years since I had been thrown out of the Commons for saying she had told a self-serving fib in relation to the Westland affair.

I told myself to behave. As we were sitting down to dinner, the conversation went like this.

'Margaret, I'm sorry your "head" was injured by that idiot who attacked your sculpture in the Guildhall.'

She replied pleasantly: 'Tam, I'm not sorry for myself, but I am sorry for the sculptor.'

Raising the soup spoon, I ventured: 'Margaret, tell me one thing – why in 800 pages …'

'Have you read my autobiography?' she interrupted, purring with pleasure.

'Yes, I have read it very carefully. Why in 800 pages did you not mention Lockerbie once?' Mrs Thatcher replied: 'Because I didn't know what happened and I don't write about things that I don't know about.'

My jaw dropped. 'You don't know. But, quite properly as Prime Minister, you went to Lockerbie and looked into First Officer Captain Wagner's eyes.'

She replied: 'Yes, but I don't know about it and I don't write in my autobiography things I don't know about.' My conclusion is that she had been told by Washington on no account to delve into the circumstances of what really happened that awful night.

Whitehall complied. I acquit the Scottish judges Lord Sutherland, Lord Coulsfield and Lord MacLean at Megrahi's trial of being subject to pressure, though I am mystified as to how they could have arrived at a verdict other than 'Not Guilty' – or at least 'Not Proven'.

As soon as I left the Colombian Ambassador's residence, I reflected on the enormity of what Mrs Thatcher had said. Her relations with Washington were paramount. She implied that she had abandoned her natural and healthy curiosity about public affairs to blind obedience to what the US administration wished. Going along with the Americans was one of her tenets of faith.

On my last visit to Megrahi, in Greenock Prison in November last year, he said to me: 'Of course I am desperate to go back to Tripoli. I want to see my five children growing up. But I want to go back as an innocent man.'

I quite understand the human reasons why, given his likely life expectancy, he is prepared, albeit desperately reluctantly, to abandon the appeal procedure.

The party of criminal war

John Pilger

John Pilger, renowned investigative journalist and documentary film-maker, is one of only two people to have twice won British journalism's top award; his television documentaries have won academy awards in both the United Kingdom and the United States. This article was originally published in the New Statesman *on 17 September 2009, and is reprinted with grateful acknowledgements.*

On the day Gordon Brown made his 'major policy speech' on Afghanistan, repeating his surreal claim that if the British army did not fight Pashtun tribesmen over there, they would be over here, the stench of burnt flesh hung over the banks of the Kunduz River. Nato fighter planes had blown the poorest of the poor to bits. They were Afghan villagers who had rushed to siphon off fuel from two stalled tankers. Many were children with water buckets and cooking pots. 'At least' 90 were killed, although Nato prefers not to count its civilian enemy. 'It was a scene from hell,' said Mohammed Daud, a witness. 'Hands, legs and body parts were scattered everywhere.' No parade for them along a Wiltshire high street.

I saw something similar in south-east Asia. An incendiary bomb had razed most of a thatched village, and bits of charred people were hanging on upended fishing nets. Those intact lay splayed and black, like large spiders.

I have never believed you need witness such a hell to comprehend the crime. A standard-issue conscience is enough for all but the morally corrupt and powerful. Fresh from another dysfunctional photo opportunity with troops in Afghanistan – a contrivance far from the impoverished suffering of that country – Brown 'authorised' the Rambo-style rescue of Stephen Farrell, a journalist of British and Irish nationality, at the site of the Nato attack. It was a stunt that went wrong. A British soldier was killed and Farrell's guide, Sultan Munadi, an Afghan journalist, was abandoned and killed. Munadi's family now fully appreciates the different worth of British and Afghan lives.

During the 1914-18 slaughter, Prime

Minister Lloyd George confided: 'If people really knew [the truth], the war would be stopped tomorrow. But of course they don't know and can't know.' Have we not yet advanced over a century's corpses to a point where the likes of Brown are denied their mendacious subterfuge? The Afghan war is a fraud. It began as an American vendetta for domestic consumption in the wake of the 11 September 2001 attacks, in which not a single Afghan was involved. The Taliban, who are Afghans, had no quarrel with the United States and were dealing secretly with the Clinton administration over a strategic pipeline. They offered to apprehend Osama Bin Laden and hand him over to a clerical court, but this was rejected.

The establishment of a permanent US/Nato presence in a resource-rich, strategic region is the principal reason for the war. The British are there because that is what Washington wants. Preventing the Taliban from storming our streets is reminiscent of President Lyndon B Johnson's plaint: 'We have to stop the communists over there [Vietnam] or we'll soon be fighting them in California.'

There is one difference. By refusing to bring the troops home, Brown is likely to provoke an atrocity by young British Muslims who view the war as a western crusade; the recent Old Bailey trial made that clear. He has been told as much by British intelligence and security services. Brown's own security adviser has said as much publicly. As with Tony Blair and the bombs of 7 July 2005, he will bear ultimate responsibility for bringing violence and grief to his own people.

More than MPs' fake expenses, it is this corrupting and trivialising of life and death that mark a fitting end to the 'modernised' Labour Party, the party of criminal war. Do the delegates preparing for the party's annual rituals in Brighton comprehend this? It says enough that most Labour MPs never demanded a vote on Blair's bloodshed in Iraq and gave him a standing ovation when he departed. One timid motion proposed by the 'grass roots' at Brighton might be allowed. This concludes that 'a majority of the public believe that the war [in Afghanistan] is unwinnable'. There is no suggestion that it is wrong, immoral and based on lies similar to those that led to the extinction of a million Iraqis, 'an episode more deadly than the Rwandan genocide', according to one scholarly estimate.

This is largely why the game of parliamentary politics is over for so many Britons, especially the young. In 2005, a bent system allowed Blair to win with fewer popular votes than the Tories in their catastrophe of 1997. New Labour's greatest achievement is the lowest turnouts since universal voting began. Today, voters watch Brown give billions of public money to casino banks while demanding nothing in return, having once hailed their practices as an inspiration 'for the whole economy'. At the recent meeting of G20 leaders in London, Brown distinguished himself by opposing, and killing, a modest Franco-German proposal for a limit on bonuses and penalties for companies that broke it. The gap between rich and poor in Britain is now the widest since 1968.

New Labour's causes and effect extend from the one in five young people denied employment, education and hope to the £12m that Blair coins in a year, 'advising' the rich and lecturing to them at £157,000 a time. For Blair's and Brown's more extreme mentors and courtiers, such as the twice-disgraced Peter Mandelson, this represents the most sought-after achievement of all: the positioning of Labour to the right of the Tories, though it is probably correct to say the two main parties have converged, competing feverishly with each other to threaten cuts in public services in order to pay for the bailing out of the banks and for the drug lords of Kabul. There is no mention of cutting the billions to be spent on replacing Trident nuclear submarines designed for the defunct Cold War.

The game is over. Corporatism and a reinvigorated militarism have finally appropriated parliamentary democracy, a historic shift. For those Afghan villagers blown to pieces in our name, one craven motion at Labour's conference is too late. At the very least, the party's 'grass roots' might ask themselves why.

Responsibility to Protest

Noam Chomsky

Professor Chomsky prepared this contribution to the UN General Assembly's Dialogue on the 'Responsibility to Protect' (R2P), which took place in New York on 23 July 2009.

The discussions about 'Responsibilty to Protect' (R2P), or its cousin 'humanitarian intervention', are regularly disturbed by the rattling of a skeleton in the closet: history, to the present moment. Throughout history, there have been a few principles of international affairs that apply quite generally. One is the maxim of Thucydides that the strong do as they wish while the weak suffer as they must. A corollary is what Ian Brownlie calls 'the hegemonial approach to law-making': the voice of the powerful sets precedents. Another principle derives from Adam Smith's account of policy-making in England: the 'principal architects' of policy – in his day the 'merchants and manufacturers' – make sure that their own interests are 'most peculiarly attended to' however 'grievous' the effect on others, including the people of England – but far more so, those who were subjected to 'the savage injustice of the Europeans', particularly in conquered India, Smith's own prime concern. A third principle is that virtually every use of force in international affairs has been justified in terms of R2P, including the worst monsters. Just to illustrate, in his scholarly study of 'humanitarian intervention', Sean Murphy cites only three examples between the Kellogg-Briand pact and the UN Charter: Japan's attack on Manchuria, Mussolini's invasion of Ethiopia, and Hitler's occupation of parts of Czechoslovakia, all accompanied by lofty rhetoric about the solemn responsibility to protect the suffering populations, and factual justifications. The basic pattern continues to the present.

The historical record is worth recalling when we hear R2P or its cousin described as an 'emerging norm' in international affairs. They have been considered a norm as far back as we want to go. The founding of this country is an example. In 1629, the Massachusetts Bay Colony was granted its Charter by the King, stating that rescuing the natives from their bitter pagan fate is 'the principal end of this plantation'. The Great Seal of the Colony depicts an Indian saying 'Come Over and Help Us'. The English colonists were thus fulfilling their responsibility to protect as they proceeded to 'extirpate' and 'exterminate' the natives, in their words – and for their own good, their honoured successors explained. In 1630, John Winthrop delivered his famous sermon depicting the new nation 'ordained by God' as 'a city on a hill', inspirational rhetoric that is regularly invoked to this day to justify any crime as at worst a 'deviation' from the noble mission of responsibility to protect.

There is no difficulty adding similar examples from other great powers in their day in the sun. It is understandable that the powerful should prefer to declare that we should forget history and look forward. For the weak, it is not a wise choice.

The skeleton in the closet made an appearance in the first case considered by the International Court of Justice sixty years ago, the Corfu Channel case. The Court determined that it 'can only regard the alleged right of intervention as the manifestation of a policy of force, such as has, in the past, given rise to most serious abuses and such as cannot, whatever be the defects in international organization, find a place in international law ...; from the nature of things, [intervention] would be reserved for the most powerful states, and might easily lead to perverting the administration of justice itself.'

The same perspective informed the first-ever meeting of the South Summit of 133 states, convened in April 2000. Its declaration, surely with the bombing of Serbia in mind, rejected 'the so-called "right" of humanitarian intervention, which has no legal basis in the United Nations Charter or in the general principles of international law'. The wording reaffirms the important UN Declaration on Friendly Relations (UNGA Res. 2625, 1970). It has been repeated since, among others by the Ministerial Meeting of the Non-aligned Movement in Malaysia in 2006, again representing the traditional victims in Asia, Africa, Latin America, and the Arab world.

The same conclusion was drawn in 2004 by the high-level UN Panel on Threats, Challenges and Change. The Panel adopted the view of the International Court of Justice and the Non-aligned Movement, concluding that 'Article 51 needs neither extension nor restriction of its long-understood scope'. The Panel added that 'For those impatient with such a response, the answer must be that, in a world full of perceived potential threats, the risk to the global order and the norm of non-intervention on which it continues to be based is simply too great for the legality of unilateral preventive action, as distinct from collectively endorsed action, to be accepted. Allowing one to so act is to allow all' – which is, of course, unthinkable.

The same basic position was adopted by the UN World Summit in 2005. While reaffirming stands that had already been accepted, the Summit also asserted the willingness 'to take collective action ... through the Security Council, in accordance with the Charter ... should peaceful means be inadequate and national authorities are manifestly failing to protect their populations' from serious crimes. At most, the phrase sharpens the wording of Article 42 on authorization for the Security Council to resort to force. And it keeps the skeleton in the closet – if, and it is a large *if*, we can regard the Security Council as a neutral arbiter, not subject to the maxims of Thucydides and Adam Smith, a matter to which I will return.

There have been efforts to draw a sharp distinction between R2P and its cousin. They may have some merit, but they go far beyond the evidence. There is a good reason why 'the right of humanitarian intervention' has been hotly contested, in substantial part along North-South lines, while R2P was affirmed – more accurately reaffirmed – by consensus at the Summit. The reason is that the Summit acceptance of R2P rhetoric adds nothing substantially new. The rights articulated in the crucial paragraphs 138 and 139 of the Summit declaration had not been seriously contested, and in fact had been affirmed and implemented, for example, with regard to apartheid South Africa. Furthermore, the Security Council had already determined that it can even use force under Chapter VII to end massive human rights abuses, civil war, and violation of civil liberties: Resolutions 925, 929, 940, June-July 1994. And as J. L. Holzgrefe observes, 'most states are signatories to conventions that legally oblige them to respect the human rights of their citizens'. The few successes of R2P that have been widely hailed, as in Kenya, had no need for the Summit resolution, though the terminology of R2P was invoked.

In substance, R2P as formulated at the South Summit is a sub-case of the 'right of humanitarian intervention', omitting the part that has been contested: the right to use force without Security Council authorization. That does not imply that there is no significance to the more explicit focus on rights that had already been widely accepted. The significance of the rhetorical shift will be determined by how it is implemented. On that matter, there are few grounds for celebration.

There have been departures from the Corfu Channel restriction and its descendants. The Constitutive Act of the African Union asserts 'The right of the Union to intervene in a Member State … in respect of grave circumstances'. That differs crucially from the Charter of the Organization of American States, which bars intervention 'for any reason whatever, in the internal or external affairs of any other state'. The reasons for the difference are clear. The OAS Charter seeks to deter intervention by the 'colossus of the North' – and has of course failed to do so. But after the collapse of the apartheid states, the African Union faced no comparable problem.

If the African Union doctrine were to extend to the OAS or NATO, then they would be entitled to intervene within their own alliances. That idea yields interesting and revealing conclusions about the OAS and NATO, which should not need elaboration. But the conclusions would be inoperative, as in the recent past, thanks to the maxim of Thucydides.

I know of only one high-level proposal to extend R2P beyond the Summit consensus and the African Union extension, namely, in the Report of the International Commission on Intervention and State Sovereignty on Responsibility to Protect (2001). The Commission considers the situation in which 'the Security Council rejects a proposal or fails to deal with it in a reasonable time'. In that case, the Report authorizes 'action within area of jurisdiction by regional or sub-regional organizations under Chapter VIII of the Charter, subject to their seeking subsequent authorization from the Security Council' ((3) E, II).

At this point, the skeleton in the closet rattles quite loudly. One reason is that the powerful unilaterally determine their own 'area of jurisdiction'. The Organization of American States and African Union cannot do so, but NATO can, and does. NATO unilaterally determined that its 'area of jurisdiction' includes the Balkans – but not NATO itself, where shocking crimes were committed against Kurds in south-eastern Turkey through the 1990s, off the agenda because of the decisive military and diplomatic support for them by the Clinton administration, with the aid of other NATO powers. NATO has also determined that its 'area of jurisdiction' extends to Afghanistan, and beyond. Secretary-General Jaap de Hoop Scheffer informed a NATO meeting in June 2007 that 'NATO troops have to guard pipelines that transport oil and gas that is directed for the West,' and more generally have to protect sea routes used by tankers and other 'crucial infrastructure' of the energy system. The expansive rights accorded by the International Commission are in practice restricted to

NATO alone, radically violating the principles of Corfu Channel and its descendants, and opening the door for resort to R2P as a weapon of imperial intervention at will.

The Corfu Channel principle provides considerable insight into both the timing of the rhetorical invocation of R2P and its cousin, and the selectivity of their application in this new incarnation. The 'normative revolution' declared by Western commentators took place in the 1990s, immediately after the collapse of the Soviet Union, which had, in earlier years, provided an automatic pretext for intervention.

The Bush Senior administration reacted to the fall of the Berlin Wall with an official exposition of Washington's new course: in brief, everything will stay much the same, but with new pretexts. We still need a huge military system, but for a new reason: the 'technological sophistication' of third world powers. We have to maintain the 'defense industrial base' – a euphemism for state-supported high-tech industry. We must maintain intervention forces directed at the Middle East energy-rich regions – where the threats to our interests that required military intervention 'could not be laid at the Kremlin's door', contrary to decades of pretense. New pretexts for intervention were needed, and the 'normative revolution' entered the stage – once again.

The natural interpretation of the timing gains support from the selectivity of application of R2P. There was of course no thought of applying the principle to the Iraq sanctions administered by the Security Council, condemned as 'genocidal' by the two directors of the oil-for-food programme, Denis Halliday and Hans von Sponeck, both of whom resigned in protest. Von Sponeck's detailed study of the horrendous impact of the sanctions has been under a virtual ban in the United States and United Kingdom, the primary agents of the programmes. Similarly, there is no thought today of protection of the people of Gaza, also a UN responsibility, along with the rest of the 'protected population' (under the Geneva Conventions), denied fundamental human rights. Nothing serious is contemplated about the worst catastrophe in Africa, if not the world: Eastern Congo, where only a few days ago, BBC reported, multinationals are once again being accused of violating a UN resolution against illicit trade of valuable minerals and thus funding the murderous conflict.

In another domain, there is no thought of invoking even the most innocuous prescriptions of R2P to respond to massive starvation in the poor countries. The UN recently estimated that the number of those facing hunger has passed a billion, while the World Food Programme of the UN has just announced major cutbacks of aid because the rich countries are reducing their meagre contributions, giving priority to bailing out banks. Several years ago UNICEF reported that 16,000 children die every day from lack of food, many more from easily preventable disease. The figures are higher now. In southern Africa alone it is Rwanda-level killing, not for 100 days, but every day. There is surely ample warning, but no thought of action under R2P, though it would be easy enough if the will were there.

In these and numerous other cases the selectivity conforms with painful precision to the maxim of Thucydides, and the expectations of the International Court of Justice 60 years ago.

Perhaps the most striking illustration of the consistent radical selectivity was in 1999, when NATO bombed Serbia, an attack featured in Western discourse as the jewel in the crown of the 'emerging norm' of humanitarian intervention, when the US was at the 'height of its glory' in leading the 'enlightened states', and the 'idealistic New World bent on ending inhumanity' opened a new era in history by acting on 'principles and values', to cite just a few of the accolades by Western intellectuals.

There are a few difficulties confronting this flattering self-image. One problem is that the traditional victims of Western intervention vigorously objected. I have already quoted the stand of the Non-aligned Movement; Nelson Mandela was particularly harsh in his condemnation. That was unproblematic: the views of the unworthy are easily ignored. Furthermore, the bombing plainly violated the UN Charter. That problem too was easily put to rest. Some resorted to legalistic maneuvering, but as the Goldstone Commission more forthrightly determined, the bombing was 'illegal but legitimate', a conclusion reached by reversing the chronology of bombing and atrocities. That leads to a third problem: the facts, which happen to be richly documented from impeccable Western sources. What they reveal is unequivocal. The NATO bombing did not end the atrocities but rather precipitated by far the worst of them, as had been anticipated by the NATO command and the White House. The conclusions that are so richly documented by the Western records are reinforced by the indictment of Milosevic, issued by the International Tribunal at the height of the bombing. With a single exception, the crimes charged follow the bombing. And we can be confident that the one pre-bombing charge – the Racak massacre – was of little principled concern to the US and Britain, if only because at the very same time they were not merely condoning but actively supporting much more serious crimes in East Timor, where the background of atrocities was incomparably more grotesque than anything that had happened in the Balkans. And that is only one of many examples right at that time.

This problem too was overcome quite simply: by virtual suppression of the ample record.

The case of East Timor is particularly instructive. On a personal note, I testified about it at the Fourth Committee in 1978, when atrocities reached the level of 'extermination as a crime against humanity committed against the East Timorese population', in the words of the later UN-sponsored Truth Commission, and Britain and France joined the US in supporting them, along with Australia and others, continuing to do so right through 1999 as atrocities sharply mounted again. After the final paroxysm of state terror in September 1999, which destroyed most of what remained of the country, National Security Adviser Sandy Berger said that the US would continue its support for the aggressors, explaining that 'I don't think anybody ever articulated a doctrine which said that we ought to intervene wherever there's a humanitarian problem'. R2P vanished in the familiar way.

To end the atrocities in this case would not have required bombing, or sanctions, or indeed any act beyond withdrawal of participation. That was demonstrated shortly after Berger's reaffirmation of Western policy, when, under strong domestic and international pressure, Clinton formally ended US participation. The invaders immediately withdrew, and a UN peacekeeping force was able to enter facing no army. That could have been done any time in the preceding quarter-century. Astonishingly, this horrendous story was soon reinterpreted as vindication of R2P, a reaction so shameful that words fail.

I mentioned that the consensus of the World Summit adheres to the Corfu principle and its descendants only if we assume that the Security Council is a neutral arbiter. It plainly is not. The Council is controlled by its five permanent members, and they are not equal in operative authority. One indication is the record of vetoes – the most extreme form of violation of a Security Council Resolution. The relevant period is from the mid-1960s, when decolonization and recovery from wartime destruction gave the UN at least some standing as representative of world opinion. Since then, the US is far in the lead in vetoes, Britain second, no one else even close. In the past quarter-century, China and France together vetoed seven resolutions, Russia six, the UK ten, and the US 45, including even resolutions calling on states to observe international law. The skeleton in the closet nods in recognition as the maxim of Thucydides strikes again.

One way to mitigate this defect in the World Summit consensus would be to eliminate the veto – incidentally, in accord with the will of most Americans, who believe that the US should follow the will of the majority and that the UN, not the US, should take the lead in international crises.

But here we run up against Adam Smith's maxim, which ensures that such heresies are unthinkable, as much so as applying R2P right now to those who desperately need protection but are not on the favoured list of the powerful.

American public opinion brings up a further consideration. The maxims that largely guide international affairs are not graven in stone, and, in fact, have become considerably less harsh over the years as a result of the civilizing effect of popular movements. For that continuing and essential project, R2P can be a valuable tool, much as the Universal Declaration of Human Rights has been. Even though states do not adhere to the Universal Declaration, and some formally reject much of it (crucially including the world's most powerful state), none the less it serves as an ideal that activists can appeal to in educational and organizing efforts, often effectively. My suspicion is that a major contribution of the discussion of R2P may turn out to be rather similar, and with sufficient commitment, unfortunately not yet detectable among the powerful, it could be significant indeed.

COMMUNICATION WORKERS UNION

Troops out of Afghanistan

Billy Hayes
General Secretary

Jane Loftus
President

Pirate's Charter

Tony Blair

In April 2009, Tony Blair returned to speak to the Chicago Council of Global Affairs, ten years after his first visit when he proclaimed his 'Doctrine of the International Community' whilst bombs rained down on Yugoslavia.

It is almost ten years to the day that I stood in this city and gave an address at the height of the Kosovo crisis. In that speech, I set out what I described as a doctrine of international community that sought to justify intervention, including if necessary military intervention, not only when a nation's interests are directly engaged; but also where there exists a humanitarian crisis or gross oppression of a civilian population.

It was a speech that argued strongly for an active and engaged foreign policy, not a reactive or isolationist one: better to intervene than to leave well alone. Be bold, adventurous even in what we can achieve.

Many, at the time, described the speech as hopelessly idealistic; dangerous even. And, probably, in the light of events since then, some would feel vindicated. As for me, I am older, better educated by the events that shaped my premiership, but I still believe that those who oppress and brutalise their citizens are better put out of power than kept in it.

However, it is undeniable that in the years that have passed, circumstances have changed radically. When I was here in 1999, Kosovo was the issue of the day, the ethnic cleansing of a civilian population, Muslims as it happened, by the Milosevic regime in Serbia. Subsequently, I authorised military action, by British forces in Sierra Leone, where a group of gangsters – portrayed in the film 'Blood Diamond' – were trying to overthrow a democratically elected Government. The gangsters were stopped, the Government saved and in late 2007, the people of Sierra Leone changed ruling party by the ballot box, and without bloodshed.

But then came Afghanistan and afterwards Iraq. Up to 11th September 2001, the military interventions, undertaken with such a humanitarian purpose, had been relatively self-contained, short in duration and plainly successful. Even after then, the removal of the Taliban Government occurred in three months. And though, of course, the reasons for that intervention were obviously justifiable by reference to a traditional view of national interest, since the Afghan regime had allowed Al Qaeda to operate training camps; the nature of the regime – its cruelty, its suppression of women, its use of the drug trade – hugely contributed to the public support for its removal.

When Saddam was ousted in 2003, even those who disagreed with the conflict could see and abhor the way he and his henchmen behaved in their barbaric treatment of their people.

However, as time has passed, so has the familiar certainty that our power would always triumph, that if the will was there, the means of intervention would be efficacious. Iraq, though measurably improved from two years ago, remains fragile; Afghanistan is proving to be a battle needing to be re-waged. Sustaining public support through so many years has proved difficult in respect of Iraq and even in respect of Afghanistan.

So: should we now revert to a more traditional foreign policy, less bold, more cautious; less idealistic, more pragmatic, more willing to tolerate the intolerable because of fear of the unpredictable consequences that intervention can bring?

My argument is that the case for the doctrine I advocated ten years ago, remains as strong now as it was then; and that what has really changed is the context in which the doctrine has to be applied. The struggle in which we are joined today is profound in its danger; requires engagement of a different and more comprehensive kind; and can only be won by the long haul. The context therefore is much tougher. But the principle is the same.

The struggle faced by the world, including the majority of Muslims, is posed by an extreme and misguided form of Islam. Our job is simple: it is to support and partner those Muslims who believe deeply in Islam but also who believe in peaceful co-existence, in taking on and defeating the extremists who don't. But it can't be done without our active and wholehearted participation.

It is one struggle with many dimensions and varied arenas. There is a link between the murders in Mumbai, the terror attacks in Iraq and Afghanistan, the attempts to destabilise countries like Yemen, and the training camps of insurgents in Somalia.

It is not one movement. There is no defined command and control. But there is a shared ideology. There are many links criss-crossing the map of Jihadist extremism. And there are elements in the leadership of a major country, namely Iran, that can support and succour its practitioners.

Engaging with Iran is entirely sensible. I fully agree with the Obama Administration in doing so. The Iranian Government should not be able to claim that we have refused the opportunity for constructive dialogue; and the stature and importance of such an ancient and extraordinary civilisation means that as a nation, Iran should command respect and be accorded its proper place in the world's affairs. I hope this engagement succeeds.

The purpose of such engagement should, however, be clear. It is to prevent Iran acquiring nuclear weapons capability; but it is more than that, it is to put a stop to the Iranian regime's policy of de-stabilisation and support of terrorism. The purpose of the engagement, as the President and Secretary of State have rightly emphasised, is not to mix the messages; but to make them indisputably clear.

Unfortunately, though, it would be rash to believe that resolving our differences with Iran's current regime, would resolve this struggle. It would, of course, be a major advance, some might argue a definitive one. But, in truth, the roots of this extremism go deep and far broader than those initiated by the Tehran revolution of 1979.

Examine, for a moment, where things stand. The future of Pakistan is critical, but uncertain. Were it to go badly wrong, the consequences would be drastic. In Lebanon, there is calm but no one doubts now the political and military might of Hezbollah. In Palestine, whatever criticism can be made of Israel, the fact remains that terrorist attacks are still aimed directly at innocent civilians who live in what is undeniably the state of Israel; and such attacks hugely impair the chance of peace on the basis of two states. And there is continuing terrorism in Iraq and Afghanistan.

These examples are well known. But how many know that in the Mindanao insurgency in the Philippines, over 150,000 have died; in Algeria, tens of thousands have perished; and as we speak, across a wide part of the northern half of Africa, previously good relations between Muslims and Christians have been sundered, and communities set against each other.

Of course, each arena of conflict has its own particular characteristics, its own origins in political or territorial disputes, its own claims and counter-claims of injustice. Of course the solution in each case will be in many respects different. But it is time to wrench ourselves out of a state of denial. There is one major factor in common. In each conflict there are those deeply engaged in it, who argue that they are fighting in the true name of Islam.

And here is the crucial point. This didn't start on 11th September 2001, or shortly before it. The roots aren't near the surface. It was in the 1970s that Pakistan's leadership decided to re-define itself through religious conviction. The storming of the Holy Mosque in Mecca took place years ago. Al Qaeda began in earnest in the 1980s. In many Arab and Muslim nations, there was more tolerance and less religiosity in the 1960s, than today. The doctrinal roots of this growing movement can be traced even further back to the period in the late 19th and early 20th century where modernising and moderate clerics and thinkers were slowly but surely pushed aside by the hard-line dogma of those, whose cultural and theological credentials were often dubious, but whose appeal lay in the simplicity of the message: Islam, they say, lost its way; the reason was its departure from the true faith as stated immutably in the 7th century; and the answer is to return to it and in doing so, vanquish Islam's foes, in the West and most especially within the ruling parties of the Islamic world itself.

The tragedy of this is that the authentic basis of Islam, as laid down in the Qur'an, is progressive, humanitarian, sees knowledge and scientific advance as a duty, which is why for centuries Islam was the fount of so much invention and innovation. Fundamental Islam is actually the opposite of what the extremists preach.

But, in recent times, as the West and nations such as China developed and opened up under the impulse of a steady, post Second World War globalisation, so these extreme elements have presented themselves in reaction to it, railing against the modern world, its evils, its decadence, its hedonistic secularism.

In terrorism, they have found a powerful, hideous and, in one sense, very modern weapon. It kills the innocent; but it does much more than that. It creates chaos in a world which increasingly works through confidence and stability.

And they have succeeded in one other sphere. They have successfully inculcated a sense of victimhood in the Islamic world, that stretches far beyond the extremes. So powerful has this become that it has severely warped the debate even in many parts of the non-Islamic world, where frequently commentators, while naturally condemning the terrorism, nevertheless imply that, to an extent, the West's foreign policy has helped 'cause' it.

President Obama's reaching out to the Muslim world at the start of a new American administration, is welcome, smart, and can play a big part in defeating the threat we face. It disarms those who want to say we made these enemies, that if we had been less confrontational they would have been different. It pulls potential moderates away from extremism.

But it will expose, too, the delusion of believing that there is any alternative to waging this struggle to its conclusion. The ideology we are fighting is not based on justice. That is a cause we can understand. And world-wide these groups are adept, certainly, at using causes that indeed are about justice, like Palestine. Their cause, at its core, however, is not about the pursuit of values that we can relate to; but in pursuit of values that directly contradict our way of life. They don't believe in democracy, equality or freedom. They will espouse, tactically, any of these values if necessary. But at heart what they want is a society and state run on their view of Islam. They are not pluralists. They are the antithesis of pluralism. And they don't think that only their own community or state should be like that. They think the world should be governed like that.

In other words, there may well be groups, or even Governments, that can be treated with, and with whom we can reach an accommodation. Negotiation and persuasion can work and should be our first resort. If they do, that's great, which is why if Hamas were to accept the principle of a peaceful two state solution, they could be part of the process agreeing it. But the ideology, as a movement within Islam, has to be defeated. It is incompatible not with 'the West' but with any society of open and tolerant people and that in particular means the many open and tolerant Muslims.

The difference, now, in the nature of any intervention, however is this. Back in April 1999, I thought that removal of a despotic regime was almost sufficient in itself to create the conditions for progress. But this battle cannot so easily be won. Because it is based on an ideology and because its roots are deep, so our strategy for victory has to be broader, more comprehensive but also more sharply defined. It is important to recognise that it is not going to be won except over a prolonged period. In this sense, it is more akin to fighting revolutionary Communism than a discrete campaign such as the one which changed the Balkans a decade ago.

So I understand completely the fatigue with an interventionist foreign policy – especially when it involves military action that takes its toll on the nation's psyche, when we see those who grieve for the fallen in battle. The struggle seems so vast, so complex, so full of layers and intersections that daunt us, that they make us unsure where we start, how we proceed and where and how on earth we end.

'Look there are people in this world who are crazy,' a friend said to me the other day, 'leave them to be crazy.' Except the problem is that they won't leave us in the comfort of our lives. That's not the way the world works today. The Holy Land, that from Tel Aviv to the River Jordan, could fit within a small US state, is many, many thousands of miles from here. But, whether there is peace there or not, will affect our peace.

So: how to win? In summary, I would identify six elements to a successful strategy.

First, we have to understand we have not caused this phenomenon but what we do now can help beat it. You can debate, in respect of Iraq or Afghanistan, whether by removing the dictatorships, we provided the terrain for terrorist organisations to work in; or the alternative view, which is that by fighting them there, we damage their capacity world-wide by focusing the battle. Whichever view is taken, there is no conceivable justification for the ghastly and wicked use of terror to kill and maim innocent people, the bulk of whom are of course Muslims. And there are ample alternatives to violence in Iraq, in Afghanistan, in the democratic process; in Palestine, Lebanon and elsewhere, in diplomacy and peaceful political change. Terror is the enemy of progress. The responsibility for terrorism lies with the terrorist and no one else.

This has to be proclaimed vigorously by us; but also upheld and shouted from the rooftops from within Islam itself.

Secondly, there is some good news. Ultimately, this battle can only be won within Islam itself and the fact is, across Islam today, we have allies. The most powerful are the ordinary people themselves. Yes, the voice of extremists may be louder. They are better organised. But they don't represent true Islam or true Muslims. We need to support these allies. We need to work with them to allow their voice to be heard and their authenticity to be established. In this regard, we should acknowledge that the world of Islam is not just the Middle East and its surrounds, but includes large parts of Asia, including Indonesia, the largest predominantly Muslim country in the world.

Third, in supporting them, we have to escape the false choice between the use of hard or soft power. Only a combination of the two will work. One of the most damaging aspects of the politics of the past ten years has been the posing of the policy challenge as between a so-called 'neo-conservative' right who were held to promulgate a purely military solution; and a so-called 'liberal' left that preferred diplomacy. Most sensible people know that here – as, in fact, in many areas of twenty-first century politics – such labels are unhelpful, counter-productive and distort the challenge. We have to fight where we are being fought against. We have to persuade where the battle is for hearts and minds.

Fourth, in the use of hard power, we have to understand one very simple thing: where we are called upon to fight, we have to do it. If we are defeated anywhere, we are at risk of being defeated everywhere. Fortunately, you can be incredibly proud of your Armed Forces here in the US, as we, the British, can be of ours. They have been in the frontline of this battle for eight long years now. They are still on it. They are brave and committed people, fighting the good fight in a cause that is right and they deserve and need our wholehearted commitment in return.

Fifth, in the deployment of soft power, we need to be likewise resolute and encompass all dimensions of the struggle. We have to be partners and helpers to the process of change and modernisation within Islam. We cannot do it. But we can support the doing of it by others. There is a perfectly intelligent view that 'imposing' democracy on Iraq and, to an extent, Afghanistan, was a mistake. It's not a view I share, obviously; but I fully respect it. However, I do not accept at all the view that democracy is unattainable or unaccepted in the Islamic world. On the contrary, eventually it is only by the embrace of greater democracy – albeit by evolution – that this battle will be won. It will be hard to accomplish. But it is the most dangerous thing imaginable, to force people to choose between an undemocratic élite with the right idea and a popular movement with the wrong one. Many of those drawn to the simplistic notion that 'Islam is the answer' are attracted because of the failure of countries to change, where change is urgently needed; and in doing so, end up agitating for the wrong change, because we are not helping sensible change to occur.

So a soft power strategy should go broad and also go deep. This extremism has many political characteristics. But it is also cloaked in religion. You can't ignore that fact. So part of defeating it lies also in religion, lies in a consistent and clear critique of its religious error by religious leaders within Islam; and in the burgeoning initiative for dialogue, understanding and action between the different faiths of the world, of which my foundation, the Tony Blair Faith Foundation, is a part. The more we reach out across the world of faith, the more common space the Abrahamic and non-Abrahamic faiths can inhabit, then the extremists and reactionaries within all faiths can be challenged.

And it needs to be organised. It needs to be at the centre of policy, properly resourced, properly serviced. It needs to go down into the education systems, ours as well as theirs, into collaboration between institutions of learning, into arts and culture. Foreign policy needs to be completely re-shaped around such a strategy.

And, of course, though I know I sound like the proverbial broken record on this, the Israel-Palestine question must be resolved. No one should suggest this dispute has caused the extremism; but its resolution would immeasurably help its defeat. It isn't a side issue; it isn't a diversion. And it is resolvable. If we understand how much it matters, we will find the will and the way to do it. But it must be done.

Finally, we are required to do something that it seems rather odd to have to say. We have to re-discover some confidence and conviction in who we are, how far we've come and what we believe in. By the way, I think this even about the economic crisis. It is severe. It's going to be really, really hard. But we will get through it and not by abandoning the market or open economic system but by learning our lessons and adjusting the system in a way that makes it better. But on any basis, this system has delivered amazing leaps forward in prosperity for our citizens and we shouldn't, amongst the gloom, forget it.

The same is true for the security threat we face. We are standing up for what is right. The body of ideas that has given us this liberty, to speak and think as we wish, that allows us to vote in and vote out our rulers, that provides a rule of law on which we can rely, and a political space infinitely more transparent than anything that went before; that body isn't decaying. It is in the prime of life. It is the future. And though the extremists that confront us have their new adherents, we have ours too, nations democratic for the first time, people tasting freedom and liking it.

And that is why we should not revert to the foreign policy of years gone by, of the world weary, the supposedly sensible practitioners of caution and expediency, who think they see the world for what it is, without the illusions of the idealist who sees what it could be.

We should remember what such expediency led us to, what such caution produced. Here is where I remain adamantly in the same spot, metaphorically as well as actually, of ten years ago, that evening in this city. The statesmanship that went before regarded politics as a Bismarck or Machiavelli regarded it. It's all a power play; a matter, not of right or wrong, but of who's on our side, and our side defined by our interests, not our values. The notion of humanitarian intervention was the meddling of the unwise, untutored and inexperienced.

But was it practical to let Pakistan develop as it did in the last thirty years, without asking what effect the madrassas would have on a generation educated in them? Or wise to employ the Taliban to drive the Russians out of Afghanistan? Or to ask Saddam to halt Iran? Was it really experienced statesmanship that let thousands upon thousands die in Bosnia before we intervened or turned our face from the genocide of Rwanda?

Or to form alliances with any regime, however bad, because they solve 'today' without asking whether they will imperil 'tomorrow'? This isn't statesmanship. It is just politics practised for the most comfort and the least disturbance in the present moment.

I never thought such politics very sensible or practical. I think it even less so now. We live in the era of interdependence; the idea that if we let a problem fester, it will be contained within its boundaries no longer applies. That is why leaving Africa to the ravages of famine, conflict and disease is not just immoral but immature in its political understanding. Their problems will become ours.

And this struggle we face now cannot be defeated by staying out; but by sticking in, abiding by our values not retreating from them.

It is a cause that must be defeated by a better cause. That cause is one of open, tolerant, outward-looking societies in which people respect diversity and difference in which peaceful co-existence can flourish. It is a cause that has to be fought for; with hearts and minds as well as arms, of course. But fought for, none the less with the courage to see it through and the confidence that the cause is just, right and the only way the future of our world can work.

Benign Whitewash

Ken Coates

During the run-up to the first Gulf War the Pope made his opinions known, and they were against the opening of hostilities. At the time I wrote to the Dalai Lama about this, seeking his opinion. He came straight out with it, very succinctly:

> 'There is no possibility of a military intervention in Tibet. As far as we all know, there is not a drop of oil to be found in the whole country.'

In this way the Dalai Lama anticipated the whole debate about humanitarian intervention, which sometimes proves possible where there are diamonds, rare metals, petroleum, or similar humanitarian considerations. This might be deemed an inadequate response to Mr. Blair, who is still harping on on his old themes. Lately he was in Chicago (23rd April 2009) telling the Council on Global Affairs that he had

> 'argued strongly for an active and engaged foreign policy, not a reactive or isolationist one: better to intervene than to leave well alone. Be bold, adventurous even in what we can achieve … I still believe that those who oppress and brutalise their citizens are better put out of power than kept in it.'

Since the British people dispensed with his services, belatedly 'putting him out of power' in June 2007, Mr. Blair very promptly enlisted as Envoy to the International Quartet to the Occupied Palestine Territories (OPT). He succeeded James Wolfensohn, who had resigned the preceding April, after accusing Israel of bad faith in maintaining its blockade of Gaza's borders and obstructing the movement of goods and persons into the territory. The Government of Israel, he said, was almost

Ken Coates is Editor of The Spokesman.

acting as if there had been no withdrawal from Gaza. Soon it was to act even more outrageously, raining phosphorus bombs on a civilian population, but there has been no hint of a Blair resignation.

The Israeli government was pleased to see a friendly face replacing that of Mr. Wolfensohn. Blair was given a mandate to mobilise assistance and foster economic development. His brief also included reform of the security apparatus of the Palestine Authority. The Quartet required the Palestine Authority to 'take strong action against Hamas and Islamic Jihad'. Benign intervention prescribed a variety of measures to crack down on leaders of the Palestinian resistance. The President of the right-wing Israeli National Union Party, Rabbi Benny Elon

> 'told a local radio station that Blair agrees with them on two primary issues. "These are uprooting the Palestinian terrorist organisations and solving the problem of the refugees without holding Israel responsible for it".'[1]

If ever there were a case for the practice of benevolent intervention, it surely arose during the subsequent Israeli offensive against Gaza. The Envoy to the Quartet studiously sat on his hands throughout the massacres.

But the persecution of Muslims in Gaza was not at the top of Blair's agenda during his speech in Chicago. No, he was concerned to vindicate his historical role in opposing the Yugoslav Government in its effort to staunch the disintegration of the country. As Blair told his audience in the Council of Global Affairs:

> 'The struggle faced by the world including the majority of Muslims, is based on an extreme and misguided form of Islam. Our job is simple: it is to support and partner those Muslims who believe deeply in Islam but also who believe in peaceful co-existence, in taking on and defeating the extremists who don't.'

One such peace-loving Muslim was Mr. Izetbegovic, at the time in question the President of Bosnia-Herzegovina. At the Tribunal which heard the case of President Slobodan Milosevic, a witness reported waiting to see President Izetbegovic in an anteroom, when an imposing figure strode in front of her for a prior appointment. It was Osama bin Laden. Osama's friendly Arab fighters were about to enlist in the Bosnian army, and all were to be issued with Bosnian passports. They could then travel freely wherever the Bosnian writ still ran. Osama bin Laden and his peace-loving friends were thus able to acquire the run of Albania, and those parts of Kosovo which were not under the control of the Yugoslav government.

It is a complicated world, and Mr. Blair's Manichean views fit it none too well. As we already reported: 'Our job is simple'.

As befits a man with a simple job, a simple mind is convenient. Mr. Blair warns us that there is a link between atrocities in Mumbai, terror attacks in Iraq and Afghanistan, the destabilisation of the Yemen, and the turbulence in Somalia. 'But is not one movement' he says. What he does not say is that the wickedness of these villains is indeed boundless, and that they can pop up as terrorists one day, and soldiers of righteousness the next. Osama, the destroyer of the Twin Towers, transforms himself into Osama the liberator of the Bosniak peoples, or Osama the hero of the Kosovars. After all, was it not Osama who earned his medals as the liberator of Afghanistan, when he drove away the evil Russians, who put all the girls in schools, and in so many ways outraged the sensibilities of the Taliban?

We always knew that Blair was a slippery customer, but as things progress we begin to see why. He lives in a world of slippery categories. This ceases to be a joke when people's lives come to depend upon his judgements.

The migration of the Mujaheddin fighters from the Middle East via Afghanistan to Bosnia involved a substantial force of men. Most had originally been armed by the Americans during the 1980s. With the establishment of an uneasy peace in Bosnia the Izetbegovic Government of Sarajevo furnished hundreds of Bosnian passports to those volunteers who chose to remain in the area. Training programmes continued under the noses of the NATO troops, and a lively trade in drugs apparently prospered.

It took time for NATO to wake up to the true alignments of its Balkan allies. General Skiaker, leaving the command of NATO troops in Kosovo, confessed that he was

> 'no longer able to see the Albanians in the area as a people "under a tyrannical regime" but rather "as a people who have frittered away world support through bickering and pettiness of mind". "No longer" said Skiaker, "is anyone willing to consider extremists as people whose grievances should be understood".' [2]

Undaunted, Tony Blair chooses to celebrate his role in the Kosovo crisis as a paradigm case of humanitarian intervention in his Chicago oration. If Bosnia and Kosovo were prototypes for what was to come, Afghanistan and Iraq were full-blown examples of the complete monstrosity of this kind of intervention. And now, since his pension depends upon it, Mr. Blair has discovered the Holy Land. This means he can afford himself the great pleasure of denouncing Iranian nuclear weapons which do not exist, whilst ignoring Israeli nuclear weapons which do exist in profusion. He can denounce Iranian terrorism, which is at least partly imaginary, whilst ignoring Israeli terrorism which is anything but imaginary.

We shall return to the question of Iraq, which has qualified Mr. Blair as a fully-fledged war criminal. The Chilcot Inquiry has been established, no doubt with the intention of applying sufficient whitewash to conceal these crimes. It may not succeed. That amount of whitewash will be very hard to find. But unfortunately, this is not a matter simply of the historical record.

The atrocities in Afghanistan continue unabated, and gather momentum. In *Spokesman* number 99, *Obama's Afghan Dilemma*, we had occasion to treat on the perfidy of the Afghan General Dostum, who after an extremely colourful and brutal career, was designated the Chief of Staff to the Commander in Chief of the Afghan Armed Forces. On February 2ⁿᵈ 2008 fifty of Dostum's goons attacked the home of Akbar Bai, who had challenged the rule of the General. He was beaten and taken prisoner, alongside his son and a bodyguard. Afghan police then surrounded Dostum's house, and liberated his captives. The Afghan Attorney General wanted to charge Dostum, accusing him of kidnapping, assault and breaking and entering. Mr. Bai, nursing serious injuries in hospital, complained that the General

'had committed a crime and must be punished if there is law and democracy in this country. This is on top of many other crimes he has committed.'

We will not repeat the remarkable dossier of these previous crimes,[3] but we will note that General Dostum (we do not at present know whether this title is now honorific or actual) has apparently returned to favour in the Afghan regime. The front page of the *Independent* newspaper on 18th August reports on the General's return from exile in Turkey, avowedly to consolidate the votes of the Uzbek community in Afghanistan behind Mr. Karzai. The Americans are reported to be aghast at this development, because President Obama is alleged to be investigating the celebrated massacre of two thousand or more Taliban captives which occurred on General Dostum's watch back in 2001. General Dostum has critics outside the international community, of course. His chief opponent in Afghanistan is the candidate who is placed third by commentators covering the Afghan Presidential election, Ramazan Bashar Dost.

'The French educated philosopher said "It is time for the international community to see that it is not acceptable that war criminals stay in power".'[4]

Mr. Blair may well emulate Lord Nelson in applying the telescope to his blind eye when considering this matter. The Afghan elections are difficult enough without raising awkward questions about General Dostum. It will be interesting to see whether President Obama has a similar facility for ignoring unpleasant facts, or whether the enquiries into Dostum's massacres will continue to be prosecuted.

The big trouble with the Afghan elections appears to be that there is considerable doubt about what constitutes a vote. Dostum will argue that the affinities of the Uzbek population follow his own example or prestige. The same cannot be said in the rest of the country. The BBC reports extensive bribery, and sharp practice on a horrifying scale.

On the *Today* programme (18th August 2009) it was reported that on this, the last day of campaigning before the voters were scheduled to go to the polls the following Thursday:

'Thousands of voting cards have been offered for sale, and thousands of dollars offered in bribes for voters.'

Ian Pannell reports:

'More than thirty candidates have spent the last four weeks crossing the country, delivering speeches and making promises. It certainly looked like a regular campaign, but there is widespread evidence that some people working for candidates have deliberately tried to influence the outcome by offering bribes, promising jobs, and actually buying votes. We were told that polling cards were being sold and were put in touch with a contact. An Afghan working for the BBC travelled to the seller's house, posing as a potential buyer. He asked for some samples as proof, then came to me. I have now been given seven voting cards. The cards show the name of the voter, his or her voting number, their details and their signature ... We were offered 500 to 1000 of these. They would be sold to us for about ten to fifteen dollars per card and it was made clear to us that there were plenty more where these came from. These are cards that would be used on election day to vote for the next President of Afghanistan.'

The BBC producer was interviewed about how such cards might be used.

'Bilal, how could these be used to benefit a candidate? Bilal: if you had, say, 1000 of these and you had someone working for a candidate at the polling station, he could in exchange give you, say, a thousand ballot papers. Interviewer: these would then go into ballot boxes in favour of your candidate? Bilal: that is correct.'

The BBC interviewer handed the cards back to the would-be seller, saying that they were not interested.

'Other people have also offered to sell us thousands of votes and some traders have even been arrested.'

In the same interview, the BBC reported on offers of substantial bribes, and a competition between rival bidders offering $10,000, $20,000, and then even more. 'I don't know where they get the money from', said the BBC's Afghan interviewee. The British Ambassador said that:

> 'Whatever the problems, it is still better than not having an election at all.'

Perhaps he should be invited to explain this at the funerals of all those eighteen-year-old boys who have been killed in order to enable an election to take place. Perhaps Mr. Blair might also wish to update his lecture to the Chicago Council on Global Affairs, explaining how benign intervention might conceivably improve election results which could otherwise make the wrong choices.

Of course, money is quite helpful in this process. This was strongly pointed out by Malalai Joya, the courageous young Afghan woman MP who has been campaigning to explain the true situation in her country. Writing in the *Independent*, on the 20th August 2009, she said:

> 'Like millions of Afghans I have no hope in the results of today's election. In a country ruled by warlords, occupation forces, Taliban terrorists, drug money and guns, no-one can expect a legitimate or fair vote … Even international observers have been speaking about widespread fraud and intimidation and, among the people on the street, there is a common refrain: the real winner has already been picked by the White House.
>
> President Hamid Karzai has cemented alliances with brutal warlords and fundamentalists in order to maintain his position. Although our constitution forbids war criminals from running for office, the incumbent has named two notorious militia commanders as his vice-presidential running mates – Karim Khalili and Mohammad Qasim Fahim, both of whom stand accused of brutalities against our people.
>
> Deals have also been made with countless fundamentalists. This week saw the return from exile of the dreaded warlord Rashid Dostum. And the pro-Iranian extremist Mohammad Mohaqiq, who has been accused of war crimes, has been promised five cabinet positions for his party in exchange for supporting Mr. Karzai.
>
> Rather than democracy, what we have in Afghanistan are backroom deals among discredited warlords who are sworn enemies of democracy and justice.
>
> The President has also continued to absolutely betray the women of Afghanistan.
>
> Even after massive international outcry – and brave protesters taking to the streets of Kabul – Mr. Karzai implemented the infamous rape law, targeting Shia women, to gain support of the fundamentalist elements in the election. He had initially promised to review the most egregious clauses, but in the end it

was passed with few amendments and the barbaric anti-women statements not removed. As Human Rights Watch recently stated: 'Karzai has made an unthinkable deal to sell Afghan women out in return for the support of fundamentalists.'

And the two main challengers to a continuation of the Karzai rule do not offer any change. Ashraf Ghani and Abdullah Abdullah are both former cabinet ministers in this discredited regime and neither has a real, broad footing among the people.

Mr. Abdullah, as the main candidate of fundamentalist warlords, has run a wide campaign with money he is receiving from the Iranian regime. He and some of the Northern Alliance commanders supporting him have threatened unrest if he loses the vote, raising fears of a return to the rampant violence and killing that marked the civil war years of the 1990s.'

How does a benign interventionist cope with this dismal state of affairs? Why, with more and stronger intervention, of course.

'My argument', says Mr. Blair, 'is that the case for the doctrine I advocated ten years ago remains as strong now as it was then; and that what has really changed is the context in which the doctrine has to be applied … [This] requires engagement of a different and more comprehensive kind; and can only be won by the long haul. The context therefore is much tougher. But the principle is the same.'

In a word, the policy generates a fiasco, the cure for which is a bigger fiasco. Are the poor Afghans to endure yet more of these traumas? Or must they wait until the electorates in Great Britain or the United States wise up and demand that the whole procedure be halted?

We do not know how many dollars the Chicago Council on Global Affairs had to subscribe in order to tap the wisdom of Mr. Blair on these matters. Doubtless he did not come cheap, and it is even possible that the votes of one or two Afghan provinces could have been purchased with such a sum.

But where does this leave the poor devils who are entrapped in this war, which generates only further turmoil and hopelessness? Liberal interventions have swept around the world in a veritable plague of death and destruction. Yugoslavia has been ravaged, but the Balkans remains at least as much of a shambles as it was before the interventionists discovered it. Iraq, which after a million of its people have been slaughtered, has declared a certain kind of peace, has celebrated it with the biggest bombs in its history, and new hecatombs of the victims. And Afghanistan is multiplying the corruption of the embezzlers by the ultimate corruption of the grave.

Postscript

Since this was written, the Afghan polls have closed, and a steady dribble of advance results and speculative predictions has run across the Western newspapers. It is evident that there has been a distinctly variable turnout, and there are serious charges about ballot stuffing and fraud. More than one candidate figures in these stories.

In the south, the turnout has sometimes been derisory, and the BBC has transmitted accounts of how in the combat zone, some polling stations were visited by one hundred-odd people out of many thousands. In the north, reported turnout is commonly much higher, but may be dubious none the less. Torn up and crumpled ballot papers which have been rejected by someone have been found in various places.

All this promoted what the BBC transcribed as an 'explosive meeting' between the outgoing President Hamid Karzai, and the American plenipotentiary, Richard Holbrooke. Holbrooke bluntly raised some of the questions about the misconduct of the polls, and fraud by a number of candidates' teams. He thought that a second round run-off could render the election process 'more credible'. Mr. Karzai apparently went ballistic, although Mr. Holbrooke twice raised the proposal to hold a second round run-off. He voiced concern about allegations that the President's own campaign team, as well as other candidates, had been behaving fraudulently and stuffing the ballot boxes. The meeting ended abruptly, although the American Embassy denied that Mr. Holbrooke had 'stormed out'. The spokeswoman did not wish to discuss the details of the meeting any further. President Karzai's spokesperson denied everything.

Two candidates have complained of attempts to defraud them of victory. The former Foreign Minister has been particularly strong in his insistence that the voting has been irregular. Early forecasts gave him an estimated thirty-eight per cent of the votes compared with forty per cent predicted for Mr. Karzai. Such a result already implies the inevitable need for a second ballot, since the winning candidate needs more than fifty per cent of the votes cast to avoid the run-off. Other candidates have polled relatively well, which makes the fifty per cent target almost impossible to obtain.

If this is true, why were there high words between the Afghan leader and President Obama's representative? What was the point? Did Mr. Karzai think that he would be able to declare victory with the figures that were already being stacked up? As the BBC reporter, Ian Pannell, said:

> 'There have been many doubts raised about the Afghan presidential election about the turnout and irregularities. But this is the first time that a leading western official has apparently expressed it quite so openly. It will raise more

questions about the credibility of the whole process, and could well make the plan to establish a meaningful government in a stable country all the harder to achieve.'

With monotonous regularity, the dead boys continue to arrive at Wootton Bassett.

References

1. Dr. Daud Abdullah: *Concerns about British and EU roles in Palestinian Authority Human Rights Abuses in the Occupied West Bank, Middle East Monitor*, p.11.
2. Cited in Lenard Cohen: *Simon Fraser University News*, November 1st 2001, volume 22, No. 5, p.3.
3. We reported them in *Spokesman* No. 77 (pp. 44-49), and in my editorial to *Spokesman* No. 99, pp. 3-14.
4. *Independent*, 18th August 2009, p.4.

* * *

'Widespread corruption and abuse of power exacerbate the popular crisis of confidence in the government and reinforce a culture of impunity. Local Afghan communities are unable to hold local officials accountable through either direct elections or judicial processes, especially when those individuals are protected by senior government officials. Further, the public perceives that the International Security Assistance Force [ISAF] is complicit in these matters ...'

'There are no clear lines separating insurgent groups, criminal networks (including the narcotics networks) and corrupt Government of the Islamic Republic of Afghanistan officials. Malign actors with the Government support insurgent groups directly, support criminal networks that are linked to insurgents, and support corruption that helps feed the insurgency ... '

Commander's Initial Assessment (General Stanley A. McChrystal)
NATO International Security Assistance Force, Afghanistan,
US Forces, Afghanistan, 30 August 2009

Kidnapped on Diego Garcia

Reprieve

Reprieve submitted a report to Parliament's Foreign Affairs Committee on 20 May 2009 (which was subsequently updated) from which these excerpts are taken. Reprieve uses the law to try to enforce the human rights of prisoners (www.reprieve.org.uk).

The question of renditions and detentions involving Diego Garcia is not new: the matter was first publicly raised in an open letter to then Prime Minister Tony Blair on 28 December 2002 when Human Rights Watch wrote:

> 'We ... urge you to take steps to ensure that torture does not take place on British soil, including the islands that are part of British Indian Ocean Territory. According to press reports in the United States, US forces are holding and interrogating suspected Al Qaeda detainees at a US operated facility on the island of Diego Garcia ... The allegations ... if true, would place the United States in violation of some of the most fundamental prohibitions of international human rights and humanitarian law ... The treatment of detainees on Diego Garcia also implicates the legal obligations of the British government ... We also urge you to request a commitment in writing from the US government as a condition of continued use of the island that it will comply with international law governing the treatment of detainees.'

In a subsequent series of questions and answers in Parliament from 2003 until 2008, the UK Government consistently denied that any detainees were on Diego Garcia, saying that the US would have to ask for UK permission to bring any detainees to the island, that the US had not done this, and that nobody was being held on or near the island. In October 2003, *Time Magazine* published a report citing interrogation records from the US prisoner Hambali that had reportedly been taken on the island, and in November 2003 the UK Bar Human Rights Committee wrote to Foreign Secretary Jack Straw raising concerns about the use of the island as well as US ships off-shore (both within and outside the 3-mile territorial limit), and specifically included a reference to 'the transit of any detainees across UK territory, for example, by landing by air on the island of Diego Garcia before being transported [off-shore]'. Over the following years further revelations would appear in the international media citing various high-level sources in the US administration concerning detentions on the island, and US officials would make public statements at best non-committal, and sometimes confirming the use of Diego Garcia for secret detentions. This would be re-iterated by well-respected international investigators at the Council of Europe and the United Nations.

In response to all of these concerns, the UK Government has consistently referred to US assurances, suggesting that there is limited British presence on, and responsibility for, the island. For example, in June 2004 the Foreign Secretary Straw stated: 'The United States authorities have repeatedly assured us that no detainees have at any time passed in transit through Diego Garcia or its territorial waters or have disembarked there and that the allegations to that effect are totally without foundation. The Government [is] satisfied that their assurances are correct.' And in its inquiry into UK involvement in renditions of July 2007, the UK Intelligence and Security Committee relied on assurances by the US government, simply stating:

'... the US has given firm assurances that at no time have there been any detainees on Diego Garcia. Neither have they transited through the territorial seas or airspace surrounding Diego Garcia. These assurances were last given during talks between US and UK officials in October 2006.'

UK presence on Diego Garcia

Why the UK should feel able to rely on US assurances alone is hard to understand, since the UK has a significant presence on Diego Garcia, and has clear civil and criminal legal jurisdiction – and obligations – when it comes to activities on the island. Diego Garcia is part of the British Indian Ocean Territory (BIOT), and is a British Overseas Territory. The UK has a significant military and administrative presence on Diego Garcia. BIOT was created by the BIOT Order of 1965. Section 4 of this Order creates a Commissioner, who has the power to make laws under Section 11. BIOT Ordinance No.3 for 1983 establishes an appellate structure, and creates a Supreme Court at Section 6. This court 'shall be a superior court of record with unlimited jurisdiction to hear and determine any civil or criminal proceedings under any law and with all the powers, privileges and authority which is vested in or capable of being exercised by the High Court of Justice in England.' The BIOT Supreme Court may sit in Diego Garcia or London, and appeal lies to the BIOT Court of Appeal and from there to the Privy Council.

Diego Garcia has its own independent administration, run by the East Africa Desk of the Foreign and Commonwealth Office in London. The Senior UK official on the island is called the British Representative, and he is there under the authority of the Foreign and Commonwealth Office. The British Representative is the Commanding Officer of Diego Garcia's civil administration, known as 'Naval Party 1002' (NP 1002). The administrative office of Diego Garcia showing US and UK flags

The British Representative is also Commander of the Royal Navy, as well as the Magistrate, the Coroner, and the Registrar of Marriages. Approximately fifty further British Royal Navy and Marines personnel work for NP 1002, carrying out policing and customs duties. A detachment of Royal Marines carries out security for the entire Chagos Archipelago …

Suspicious flights confirmed by David Miliband

Finally, in February and July 2008, Foreign Secretary Miliband stated that two prisoners had been rendered through Diego Garcia, despite previous US assurances that this had never happened.

On 21 February 2008, UK foreign secretary David Miliband conceded by statement to Parliament and by letter to Clive Stafford Smith [of Reprieve] that two rendition flights carrying US prisoners had stopped on Diego Garcia, in January and September 2002. By statement to Parliament, Mr Miliband said,

> 'Contrary to earlier assurances that Diego Garcia had not been used for rendition flights, recent US investigations have now revealed two occasions, both in 2002, when this had in fact occurred. An error in the earlier US records search meant that these cases did not come to light. In both cases a plane with a single detainee on board refuelled at the US facility in Diego Garcia. The detainees did not leave the plane, and the US government has assured us that no US detainees have ever been held on Diego Garcia or any other Overseas Territory or through the UK itself since then.'

In an email message obtained by ABC News and the Associated Press, CIA Director-General Michael Hayden made a statement limited only to 'refuelling' on Diego Garcia:

> 'The refuelling, conducted more than five years ago, lasted just a short time. But it happened. That we found this mistake ourselves, and that we brought it to the attention of the British government, in no way changes or excuses the reality that we were in the wrong. An important part of intelligence work, inherently urgent, complex, and uncertain, is to take responsibility for errors and to learn from them … Our government had told the British that there had

been no rendition flights involving their soil or airspace since 9/11. That information, supplied in good faith, turned out to be wrong.'

In respect of the individuals on board, David Miliband said on 21 February 2008:

> 'The House will want to know what has become of the two individuals in question. There is a limit to what I can say, but I can tell the House the following. The US government has told us that neither of the men was a British national or a British resident. One is currently in Guantanamo Bay. The other has been released.'

Since then, despite pledging to 'work through the details and implications of this information,' the UK has done nothing further to clarify the situation, except that, on 12 February 2009, the Foreign Minister responded to a parliamentary question from Andrew Tyrie MP, saying that the prisoner who was previously stated to have been in Guantanamo Bay had since been released:

> **Mr. Tyrie**: To ask the Secretary of State for Foreign and Commonwealth Affairs whether one of the detainees rendered through Diego Garcia is still being held in the Guantanamo Bay detention centre.
>
> **Bill Rammell**: Both of the individuals rendered through Diego Garcia in 2002 have been returned to their countries of nationality.

However, the UK government declined to conduct a proper investigation into these revelations, and merely invited non-governmental organisations and MPs to submit questions regarding further suspicious flights. The result was inevitable: Mr Miliband announced in July 2008 that the US had assured Britain that no further instances of rendition had been found.

The UK Foreign and Commonwealth Office must urgently clarify:

- *What is the scope and terms of the FCO's 'inquiry' into renditions, and is the inquiry ongoing?*
- *How long has it known the identities, rendition history and current situation of the people concerned;*
- *Why has it not released this information?*
- *What assurances, if any, have been sought by the British and/or granted by the Americans in relation to these individuals, and when?*

Identifying the prisoners

In identifying the two prisoners referred to, we have been given limited information by the British government ... It should be noted by the Committee that there have been many more credible allegations of specific prisoners being held on the island, including 'High Value Prisoners'

Hambali, Abu Zubaydah and Khaled Sheikh Mohammed, all now being held in Guantanamo Bay. The United States government has admitted that 'advanced interrogations techniques' – essentially a euphemism for torture – were used on this category of prisoners, and it has also been admitted that Abu Zubaydah and Khaled Sheikh Mohammed were 'waterboarded' on numerous occasions whilst they were held in US custody. Because of limited resources, for the purposes of this submission we have limited ourselves to an investigation of just one of the prisoners on the rendition flights conceded by David Miliband in February 2008 [who was identified by a process of elimination]. We hope that an examination of this case will also serve to highlight the very many questions that have been left unanswered by the Foreign Secretary in the matter of Diego Garcia.

Muhammed Saad Iqbal Madni

Mohammed Saad Iqbal Madni was detained in Jakarta on 9 January 2002, reportedly at the request of the CIA. According to the *Washington Post*, US authorities urged the Indonesians to apprehend him after they claimed to have discovered a link to Richard Reid, the so-called British 'shoe bomber'. On 11 January 2002, with no judicial oversight of his transfer, Madni describes being pushed aboard an unmarked, US-registered Gulfstream V jet at a military airport in Jakarta, and taken to Cairo. Madni spent 92 torturous days in Cairo before being taken to Bagram Airforce Base and then Guantanamo Bay, where he remained until his release in August 2008. The London *Guardian* reported on Madni's case as early as March 2002, when Madni was still being tortured in Egypt:

'Madni was taken from Indonesia to Egypt on a US-registered Gulfstream jet without a court hearing after his name appeared on al-Qaida documents. He remains in custody in Egypt and has been subjected to interrogation by intelligence agents.'

Regarding the apparent reason for his apprehension, Madni has persistently denied any connection with Richard Reid. In his Combatant Status Review Tribunal he maintained that he was betrayed by one of four radical Islamists whom he met by accident on a trip to Indonesia in November 2001 to deal with family business after his father's death:

'After I went to Indonesia, I got introduced to some people who were not good. They were bad people. Maybe I can say they were terrorists. When someone gets introduced to someone, it is not written on their foreheads that they are bad or good.'

This account is corroborated by a *Washington Post* investigation, which found that during his time in Jakarta, Madni had spent 'hours on end watching television at a friend's house,' and when he was not doing that, handing out business cards 'identifying him as a Koran reader for an Islamic radio station'. The *New York Times* reported that the entire, embarrassing basis for Madni's capture, rendition and torture was that Madni was, in the words of one of his uncles, a young man who 'had a childish habit of trying to portray himself as important', and had simply made something up, that bombs could be hidden in his shoes, to impress his new friends in Jakarta. The comment was picked up by Indonesian intelligence agents, who were monitoring the men, and relayed to the CIA, who decided to pick Madni up after Richard Reid's failed shoe bomb attack a few weeks later. A US intelligence official speaking to the *New York Times* confirmed Madni's uncle's account, calling Madni a 'blowhard' who 'wanted us to believe he was more important than he was'. Thus, Madni's seven-year journey through the secret prison system was based on a single ill-advised comment.

Mohammed Saad Iqbal Madni was seized at 4am on 9 January 2002, in Jakarta, Indonesia. During the evening of 10 January 2002, Madni says that he was bundled aboard a plane at an airport in Jakarta, which took off around 10pm. A *Washington Post* report of March 2002 speaks of eye-witnesses at that time seeing a man being bundled aboard an unmarked, US-registered Gulfstream V jet at a military airport in Jakarta, which took him to Cairo. This is further corroborated by Eurocontrol flight-logs, which were not released until many years after the first reports of Madni's rendition, showing the movements of a well known rendition plane Gulfstream V with tail-number N379P, which has been dubbed 'the torture taxi' by journalists and plane spotters around the world. The logs show that N379P left Washington at 16:47 on 9 January 2002, arriving in Cairo at 03:32 in the morning of 10 January 2002. According to *The Sunday Times*, N379P collected some Egyptian security personnel and flew them to Cairo to assist with the rendition of Madni.

The *New York Times*, which published an interview with Madni soon after his release in August 2008, reports that 'during the flight to Cairo, Mr. Iqbal said, he was bleeding from his nose, mouth and ears, and was unable to move because shackles wound tightly around his body.'

Madni has since told Reprieve that the plane stopped over once en-route to Egypt, and that people took photographs of him at that point: 'the plane did stop for thirty minutes en route to Cairo'. He was hooded and some cameramen came into the plane and took pictures of him. He remembers the camera flashes. He was never taken out of the plane. Madni's recollection of being photographed during his rendition is consistent with the accounts of other rendition victims.

The time taken from Jakarta to this place was about 5 to 7 hours and then it was another 3 or 4 hours to Cairo. The distance from Jakarta to Diego Garcia is 3,797 km (2,359 miles or 2,050 nautical miles). N379P had an average range of 5,800 nautical miles, cruising at between 459 and 585 knots. At 470 knots, then, the flight duration is consistent with Madni's estimate that the first leg of the flight took 5-7 hours. The distance from Diego Garcia to Cairo is 6,032 km (3,748 miles or 3,257 nautical miles). Again, Madni's recollection of the flight duration of 3-4 hours for this second leg, including a stop-over of around 30 minutes, is consistent with the above average cruising speed of N379P. And, in the long flight across the Indian Ocean from Jakarta to Cairo, a stop-over on Diego Garcia would be eminently logical: as the grandfather of the unsuccessful 2008 presidential candidate, US Admiral John S McCain (1884–1945,) once put it, 'as Malta is to the Mediterranean, Diego Garcia is to the Indian Ocean – equidistant from all points'.

The UK Foreign and Commonwealth Office must urgently clarify:

● *When did the UK government become aware of the apprehension of Mohammed Saad Iqbal Madni, or of an individual believed at the time to be a close associate of Richard Reid;*
● *If they knew about Mr Madni's apprehension at the time that he was transferred through Diego Garcia;*
● *If and when any British personnel saw or spoke to Mr Madni whilst he was being transferred through Diego Garcia or at any time between his apprehension in January 2002 and his release in August 2009.*

Imprisonment and torture in Egypt

Madni says he arrived in Egypt on 11 January 2002, at 11:30am. When the plane landed, he was told he was in Cairo. He was assigned a basement room like 'a grave', about 6 feet by 4 feet, he said, and was kept there for 92 torturous days. In an interview with the *New York Times*, Madni said that on January 11, 12 and 20, 2002, he was interrogated for 12 to 15 hours on each occasion. He described his interrogators as Egyptians, but also noted that there were other men in the room whose faces were covered and who did not speak, but who passed notes with questions to the Egyptians.

Eurocontrol flight logs show that Madni's rendition plane stopped over in Cairo for six days after dropping him, before returning to Washington via Prestwick, again utilizing UK territory. It is possible therefore that some of the US rendition crew were the masked men Madni describes being present at the interrogations on 11 and 12 January 2002, before flying home.

Madni told the *New York Times* that his Egyptian captors tried to torture a confession out of him, and that when he told them that he had never been to Afghanistan nor had he met Usama Bin Laden, they responded by giving him electric shocks and forcing him to take drugs: 'I cry and I yell,' he said. 'Also they gave me brain electric shocks.' He said he was forced to consume liquids that were laced with drugs 'so you don't know what you are talking about'…

The UK Foreign and Commonwealth Office must urgently:

- *Clarify if and when the British government sought assurances from the US or Egyptian government as to Mr Madni's treatment whilst he was in Egypt;*
- *Reveal all records and communications, including flight-logs, flight manifests and any other records, corroborating Madni's account of his illegal detention and torture in Egypt;*
- *Request from the US government any records and communications, including photographs, corroborating Madni's account of his illegal detention and torture in Egypt.*

Afghanistan

Madni told Reprieve that in April of 2002, the Americans flew him to Bagram, the American air base outside the Afghan capital, Kabul. Again, Eurocontrol flight-logs exactly match Madni's recollection. This time, Madni was flown via a joint US/German airbase near Tashkent, where he changed planes before being taken on to Bagram.

In an interview with the *New York Times*, Madni describes being held in Bagram for almost a year for further interrogation. Madni said that in Bagram he was shackled and handcuffed in a small cage with other detainees, and for a period of six months, shifted from cell to cell every few hours so that he was deprived of sleep. In Bagram, his interrogators were still intent in extracting a confession: 'A CIA person said, "We forgive you; just accept you met Osama bin Laden." I said, "No, I'm not going to say that".'…

The UK Foreign and Commonwealth Office must urgently:

- *Clarify if and when the British government sought assurances from the US government as to Mr Madni's treatment whilst he was in Afghanistan;*
- *Reveal all records and communications, including flight-logs, flight manifests and any other records, corroborating Madni's account of his*

illegal detention and torture in Afghanistan;
- *Request from the US government any records and communications, including photographs, corroborating Madni's account of his illegal detention and torture in Afghanistan.*

Guantánamo

Madni arrived at Guantánamo on March 23, 2003. It is evident from accounts of fellow prisoners that Madni was in a particularly bad mental and physical state in Guantánamo. Rustam Akhmyarov [a Russian detainee] recalled that he 'was passing blood in his faeces,' and recalled that he overheard US officials telling him, 'we will let you go if you tell the world everything was fine here'. Mamdouh Habib has confirmed Akhmyarov's analysis, recalling how Madni had 'pleaded for human interaction'. He said that he overheard him saying, 'Talk to me, please talk to me … I feel depressed … I want to talk to somebody … Nobody trusts me.' On the 191st day of his incarceration, according to Madni's own account, he attempted to commit suicide. Habib remembers that at Guantánamo Madni became so depressed he tried to hang himself twice, and went on three hunger strikes.

British citizens released in 2004, Rhuhel Ahmed, Asif Iqbal and Shafiq Rasul, also recalled Madni in Guantánamo, saying that 'he had had electrodes put on his knees', and 'something had happened to his bladder and he had problems going to the toilet,' but explained that he had been told by interrogators that he would not receive treatment unless he co-operated with them, in which case he would be 'first in line for medical treatment'. In a 2007 court filing to Washington Court of Appeals, Dr. Ronald L. Sollock, the commander of the Naval Hospital at Guantánamo Bay, reveals that from 2003 Madni was prescribed antibiotics, and that in April 2007 he was diagnosed with a perforated left eardrum, inflammation of the left external ear canal and inflammation of the left middle ear.

The UK Foreign and Commonwealth Office must urgently:
- *Clarify if and when the British government sought assurances from the US government as to Mr Madni's treatment whilst he was in Guantánamo;*
- *Reveal all records and communications, including flight-logs, flight manifests and any other records, corroborating Madni's account of his illegal detention and torture in Guantánamo;*
- *Request from the US government any records and communications, including photographs, corroborating Madni's account of his illegal detention and torture in Guantánamo.*

Mr Madni's release

Madni finally returned home to Pakistan in August 2009. After Guantánamo, Madni was flown on an American military aircraft to Islamabad airport, where two American Embassy officers, First Lt. Brian Strait and Keith Easter, witnessed his release, according to a United States government document he displayed. He was admitted to a hospital in Islamabad for treatment, and then questioned for three weeks at a safe house by Pakistani intelligence officers ... Pakistani security officers then drove him back to Lahore and his extended family. 'It was like a new life for me,' he said. 'I was born again. There is no word to explain.'

As a result of his experience in US secret prisons, Mr Madni is now unable to walk unaided ...

UK knowledge of the rendition programme

Mohammed Saad Iqbal Madni is an Egyptian national, and this fact may go some way to explaining the speed of his transfer – one of the first reported – as well as the apparently seamless co-operation between the US, Egyptian and UK authorities in his abduction in the otherwise chaotic months after 9/11.

'Post 9/11' transfer to torture and US military and CIA detention has its roots in the early 1990s when, under President Clinton, express policies were formulated allowing for the extra-legal apprehension and transfer of terrorist suspects. In practice, in the early years this programme largely but not exclusively involved US-assisted delivery of Egyptian Islamists back to Egypt, where they routinely faced incommunicado detention, torture and often death. At its inception, when he was rendered from Jakarta via Diego Garcia to Cairo, Mohammed Saad Iqbal Madni's transfer resembled one of these earlier Egyptian renditions, and it was therefore a procedure that the British would have been familiar with.

Indeed, Madni's case is demonstrative of the way that the US secret prison system grew out of existing practices and arrangements with partner-states such as Egypt, with the help of co-operating states such as the UK. Whilst the rendition programme would expand in the years following the invasion of Afghanistan to involve many new partners, the US's strong relationships with Egypt would remain, as demonstrated by the large number of prisoners of many nationalities sent to Egypt for torture in the years following the invasion of Afghanistan. It is inconceivable that the UK was not aware of the 'pre-9/11' rendition programme that was operating throughout the 1990s, involving transfers indistinguishable from Madni's rendition: there were numerous public statements by US officials about the programme at the time, and in 2006 Jack Straw conceded to the UK Parliament that permission had been sought by the US for five renditions in 1998 alone, through UK territory.

And it is inconceivable that the UK was not aware that, in the months following 9/11, the rendition programme accelerated, and broadened in scope. According to media reports, a few days after the 9/11 attacks, the White House issued a new directive – still classified – giving the CIA wide powers to carry out renditions without White House approval for each individual case. Like earlier cases, renditions post 9/11 have involved both US and foreign state territory and the transfer of foreign nationals to third countries by 'host' states, facilitated by US aircraft and/or personnel. Excluding renditions from Afghanistan to Guantánamo Bay, of which there were hundreds by the end of 2002 that routinely crossed European airspace, according to US security sources, at least 150-200 renditions occurred between 9/11 and 2004. Cases that have come to light since 2001 reveal that since 9/11, individuals have been rendered by the US to a wide list of states including Syria, Egypt, Morocco, Saudi Arabia, Jordan, Pakistan and Uzbekistan.

During the months between September 2001 and January 2002 when Madni was apprehended, at least five high-profile rendition cases were reported in the international media. These cases included: on 12 and 14 December 2001, Abu Faisal and Abdul Aziz were reportedly arrested in Pakistan by the US; on 11 November 2001, Ibn Al-Shaykh al-Libi was reportedly arrested in Pakistan; and in January 2002, suspected commander of Al Qaeda training camp Abd al-Hadi al-Iraqi was reportedly arrested. In January of 2002, the US was cranking itself into full swing with preparations for a series of mass renditions from Afghanistan to Guantanamo Bay, as well as renditions far from the 'theater of war' to the Cuban prison. The first military cargo plane to Guantánamo Bay, carrying at least two UK nationals, arrived in Guantánamo from Afghanistan on 20 January 2002, and on 19 January 2002, six Algerian men had been rendered by US agents from Bosnia to Guantánamo Bay despite being released by the Bosnian Supreme Court for lack of evidence, and despite an injunction from the Bosnian human rights chamber that four of them be allowed to remain in the country pending further proceedings. By January 2002 when Mr Madni was rendered through Diego Garcia, the UK was already actively involved in what would become an accelerating pattern over the next three-four years, with a strong presence on the ground in Afghanistan, and evident involvement from the latter months of 2001 in the illegal detention process of their own nationals.

UK knowledge and possible cover-up of Mr Madni's rendition flight

The 1976 Exchange of Notes between the UK and US Governments in relation to Diego Garcia clearly requires that the UK must be informed of all intended movements of US ships and aircraft on or through BIOT territory, stating at paragraph 3: 'The US Commanding Officer and the Officer in Charge of the United Kingdom Service element shall inform each other of intended movements of ships and aircraft'. In addition, the UK Foreign Office has stated that the United States would need to ask the permission of the UK should it bring any 'unlawful combatants' onto the island. Despite this, it has been extremely difficult to obtain any flight records involving Diego Garcia. In response to questions about why the two flights conceded by David Miliband in February 2008 had taken so long to come to light, former Foreign Secretary Margaret Beckett has said, 'It was very difficult for the government to go back and look at what had happened on previous occasions. There was not a clear, simple trace of record keeping. That may, I don't know, have been the case in the United States also.' Why, we might well ask, is there not a simple trace of record keeping? It cannot be that complicated to keep records on aircraft coming through the base – indeed, it is required, and done routinely by air traffic controllers. Worryingly, more than one independent source has since suggested that there had been logs of flights through Diego Garcia but the logs had since been destroyed.

An examination of detailed records available for four other rendition flights conducted by N379P reveal that the plane routinely operated under various 'special status designators' (STS indicators) that might go some way towards explaining the difficulties in tracing records referred to by Margaret Beckett. If it were found that these STS indicators had been used for Mr Madni's flight, this might explain in part why conventional records do not appear to have been easily available. Further, and more importantly, if found to have been used in the course of Madni's rendition flight (and if they were not, this would have been a departure from the norm), these STS indicators would indicate both knowledge of and authorisation for the rendition at the highest echelons of both the US and the UK governments, since by their very nature the special status designators in question would indicate that the flights were being planned and executed with the full collaboration of the operating state (in this case the United States), and the 'host' states through which the aircraft travelled (in this case, the United Kingdom).

An examination of available 'data-string' flight records for the renditions on N379P of Bisher Al-Rawi, Jamil El-Banna, Binyam Mohamed and Mohamedou Ould Slahi reveals that in the course of all four rendition operations, N379P at various times declared itself to have the special status 'STS/STATE'. The prerequisite for this designation is clear: 'Only those flights ... that are specifically required by the State Authorities, e.g. military or civil registered aircraft used in military, customs and police services, shall use the sub-field STS/STATE indicator'. For these flights, in other words, the operators were claiming an official status for N379P as an aircraft on state duty, only one category below the aircraft that carry Heads of State [STS/HEAD].

In addition, in the course of all four renditions, the operators of N379P also declared the plane to have the special status 'ATFMEXEMPT'. This STS designator is even more strictly limited, because once granted it allows deviations from planned routes and other important exemptions. In invoking this status, the aircraft was thereby exempted from adhering to the normal rules of air traffic flow management (ATFM), and did not, for example, have to wait at airports for approved departure slots. Invoking this designation effectively allowed N379P to fly wherever it liked, whenever it liked, without having to file new flight-plans. Crucially though, flights can only be granted this special status when they are 'specifically authorised by the relevant national authority' – a requirement that appears to be taken very seriously – since such exemptions are only granted when 'specifically authorised by the relevant national authority'. The demonstrably complete ease of movement and lack of any evident record trail as N379P delivered Madni to torture in Cairo indicates that this designation may well have been wrongfully used to facilitate this rendition. Wrongful use of this designation in the course of Madni's rendition flight would point to a significant degree of British complicity in the operation: as put by the investigator for Council of Europe Senator Dick Marty,

> 'Both of these "special status" designations invoked for the aircraft N379P ... vouch for the prior knowledge and collaborative planning input of the states whose territory or airspace was being traversed, because such exemptions "shall only be used with the proper authority". Indeed, such is the strictness with which these designations are invoked and approved, every flight operator's manual accessed by the consultant emphasizes the limitations on their use. '

In addition to any wrongful usage of 'STS designators', N379P may have also been operating under a military travel order, categorised as the sort of military flight governed by the unpublished NATO agreements of 4 October 2001, in which NATO allies 'agreed today – at the request of the United States – to take eight measures, individually and collectively, to expand the options available in the campaign against terrorism'. Only two of the eight measures set out in the agreement have been made public:

(1) Blanket overflight clearances for the United States' and other Allies' aircraft for military flights related to operations against terrorism,

(2) Blanket access to ports and airfields on NATO territory, including for refuelling, for United States and other Allies for operations against terrorism.

If N379P were operating under such an order, it is not clear that specific permission would be sought for any particular flight, rather some form of procedural notification may have sufficed. In keeping with the secrecy of most of the agreement, the nature of any records that may or may not have been created is similarly opaque. In addition, given the above agreement, it is also possible that, after 4 October 2001, such operations could have come to be regarded as 'routine' by the US and the UK. It may be the case that under the law in Diego Garcia, 'routine' military operations may be exempted from relatively burdensome procedure, merely requiring some form of notification rather than a request for permission. This could again possibly affect the nature of any records that may or may not have been created.

Finally, Jeppesen [the aircraft operator] may also have filed false flight logs for N379P, in the course of Madni's rendition circuit. The Council of Europe has found that Jeppesen did so for the same plane in its numerous clandestine trips in and out of Poland:

'The aviation services provider customarily used by the CIA, Jeppesen International Trip Planning, filed multiple 'dummy' flight plans for many of these flights. The 'dummy' plans filed by Jeppesen – specifically, for the N379P aircraft – often featured an airport of departure (ADEP) and/or an airport of destination (ADES) that the aircraft never actually intended to visit. If Poland was mentioned at all in these plans, it was usually only by mention of Warsaw as an alternate, or back-up airport, on a route involving Prague or Budapest, for example. Thus the eventual flight paths for N379P registered in Eurocontrol's records were inaccurate and often incoherent, bearing little relation to the actual routes flown, and almost never mentioning the name of the Polish airport where the aircraft actually landed – Szymany.'

Again, this unconventional behaviour from N379P involved not only the private company Jeppesen Trip-planning, but also a State party, in this case

Poland, in the practical form of the Polish Aviation Authority (PANSA). Given the almost total absence of available flight logs for suspicious flights through Diego Garcia, as well as its obvious strategic significance for both the US and the UK, it is not beyond the realm of possibility that something similar has happened in the case of flights through Diego Garcia.

The UK Foreign and Commonwealth office must urgently reveal:

- *All internal UK government, military and other communications and records relating in any way to flights through or transfers of prisoners through Diego Garcia;*
- *All communications and records between the UK government or military, and any foreign government or military, relating in any way to flights through or transfers of prisoners through Diego Garcia;*
- *How many flight logs were destroyed, and what was their content;*
- *What is the routine practice for destruction of such records;*
- *When were these particular records destroyed;*
- *Why were these particular logs destroyed;*
- *When were the first questions posed about the rendition flights;*
- *Had they been destroyed by the time that questions were regularly being asked about rendition flights;*
- *Who authorised the destruction of these logs, and who was aware of the decision either at the time or later.*

As Mr Madni's case unfolds, many more questions are raised than answered about Diego Garcia and Britain's role in US detentions. Against the backdrop of emerging evidence of UK knowledge and involvement in all corners of the global US secret prison system, UK claims to ignorance appear increasingly difficult to accept. It is time for the UK government to finally come clean about its role in Mr Madni's detention, and to reveal precisely who else has been held on and rendered through Diego Garcia, what happened to them there, and where they are now.

A New World
at the Globe

Ann Talbot

Trevor Griffiths

Ann Talbot reviews A New World: A Life of Thomas Paine *by Trevor Griffiths, which continues its run at Shakespeare's Globe in London until 9 October. She interviewed Trevor Griffiths in* Spokesman 101, *and also reviewed his original screenplay about Paine, entitled* These are the Times. *She writes for the World Socialist Web Site (www.wsws.org).*

Trevor Griffiths' lyrics of the songs for A New World *follow the review. The original music for the songs is composed by Stephen Warbeck.*

Trevor Griffiths' *A New World: A Life of Thomas Paine* brings to the stage an eighteenth century figure who made a significant contribution to both the American and French revolutions, and whose writings have continued to influence revolutionary movements ever since. Griffiths' play will introduce thousands to Thomas Paine, the man who wrote *The Rights of Man,* in defence of the French Revolution, *Common Sense,* and *The American Crisis*, which was read to Washington's troops on the eve of the battle of Trenton and marked a turning point in the War of Independence.

We follow Paine over a 30 year period, as Griffiths takes us from his emigration to America in 1774 to his death in 1809. This is a large slice of time to fit into one evening, and covers epochal events, but Griffiths deftly knits biography and history together in a play which engages both the intellect and the emotions of its audience. This is a play which takes its subject seriously, and takes its audience seriously.

Paine is often referred to as the forgotten Englishman, but he was a citizen of both America and France, and it would be more accurate to regard him as a citizen of the world. Some people are forgotten because their ideas have a diminishing relevance or because their celebrity was a superficial feature of a particular age, but Paine's ideas have not sunk into a natural and deserved oblivion. His neglect is a much more constructed phenomenon that expresses just what an uncomfortable figure he remains in a period when many of the social inequalities and forms of oppression about which he wrote still exist or have taken on new forms.

Paine was born in Thetford, Norfolk in 1737. Leaving school at the age of 12, he was apprenticed as a staymaker, and later became an excise man in Lewes, Sussex. By the time he sailed for America he was bankrupt, had no settled employment and, apparently, no prospects. What made the penniless man into Thomas Paine was the revolutionary crisis that was reaching its peak as he disembarked. Griffiths is right to choose this as the start for his play. This is the point at which Paine steps into history and, as Griffiths shows, it is even when he gets his name because a printer adds an 'e' to it in his first published article.

Print shops figure largely in *A New World*. There is the printers' shop of the *Pennsylvania Magazine* and, later, we see Paine in the Paris print shop of the revolutionary paper *La Bouche de Fer*. These are not merely background scenes, they are part of Paine's character. Arriving in Pennsylvania he is a working man, confident enough of his skill to negotiate a job for himself in this new world. In Paris we see the physical effort it takes to bring out a thrice weekly paper in the tired bodies of the revolutionaries asleep alongside their press. Griffiths gives a tangible sense of the importance of papers, pamphlets and magazines to these first modern revolutions, and of the role that Paine played as a writer in giving voice to social layers that were normally excluded from political life.

Griffiths' play is an adaptation of the screenplay he wrote for Richard Attenborough, who has long planned to film the life of Thomas Paine. Griffiths published it as *These are the Times: a Life of Thomas Paine* in 2005 (see www.spokesmanbooks.com) when it seemed that the film would never be made. Since then it has been adapted as a BBC radio play and now for the stage. The changes Griffiths has made for the stage are far greater than those in the radio play. Not least he has had to cut one and a half hours from the text. Yet Paine the writer emerges from that process more clearly defined. In the screenplay Paine wears a wooden pen in his jacket lapel to indicate his trade. In the play the physical presence of the press on the stage makes the same statement.

For a man who spent so much of his time in the thick of often frantic activity, there is a certain loneliness and isolation about Paine. It is in part the result of a patchy and heavily biased historical record, but also probably expresses something about the nature of Paine as a writer. There are points at which Paine the writer and Griffiths the writer shade into one another. All writers must inevitably use themselves and their own experience as the basis for any character they create, but Griffiths' depiction of Paine takes on the character of a protracted examination of the writer's relationship to the dominant theme of Griffiths' own work – revolution.

John Light who plays Thomas Paine conveys this sense of containment and reserved passion with great skill. He reveals most about the inner feelings of his character in his interaction with the child characters Lotte, played by Julia Reinstein, and Will (Daniel Anthony), and the three women in Paine's life, Philly (Jade Williams), Marthe (Laura Rogers) and Carnet played by Alix Riemer.

With the children the almost child-like innocence of Paine's own character emerges. Their quest for knowledge is his. Will, a slave boy, accompanies Paine through the streets of Philadelphia as a younger equal bearing his globe from one set of lodgings to another. In one of the most powerful moments of the play Paine returns to Philadelphia to find that Will has been hung by the British. The dramatic effect is all the greater because it takes place among the standing spectators in the yard of the theatre. The Globe is a reconstruction of Shakespeare's Globe and seems to have given Griffiths possibilities in adapting his screenplay for the stage that a more conventional modern theatre could not. The actors push their way through the crowd as though the audience were participants in the scene.

The female characters each have their own story. Griffiths has created three dimensional women whose struggles provide painful insights into the impact of class society on those whom it oppresses. Paine relates to each woman as an equal, and each responds in her own way. Philly, the abused prostitute, saves his life when he is carried off the ship at Philadelphia sick with fever. Marthe makes a fair copy of *Common Sense*, but cannot accept a relationship that is not sanctioned by society. Of the three, only Carnet can respond freely to Paine. Riemer's portrayal lit up the stage.

One of the finest scenes involves the French revolutionary Danton, vividly realised by James Garnon, making a speech to the Cordeliers Club – in French – while Carnet, thinly disguised as a man, simultaneously translates for Paine. The scene conveys in seconds the elemental character of a revolution. What a film would have shown in expensive crowd scenes, Griffiths and director Dominic Dromgoole have achieved with far greater economy of resources.

Central to Griffiths' achievement is his ability to create characters who are rooted in the history of the period, but psychologically credible and moving to a modern audience. He is able to carry the audience through the historical complexities of the period without being didactic because the issues which arise are issues for the characters themselves. Paine and Jefferson (Jamie Parker) discuss the drafting of the Declaration of Independence against the background of fidgeting children. Paine and

Danton discuss the nature of revolution while the great orator dresses and applies kohl to his eyes to increase the dramatic effect of the speech he is about to make. One has the sense that these characters are grappling with these great questions of modern history for the first time. With Griffiths, history is not something that happened and about which he is going to inform us; it is something which unfolds each night at the Globe.

His achievement in adapting a work written for the highly naturalistic medium of film to the stage is considerable. He achieves it with a mastery of his art that obscures the complexity of the task. He has used song, the music is by Steven Warbeck, and extended the role of Benjamin Franklin, played to great effect by Keith Bartlett, as a narrator. Neither of these techniques seems forced. They draw the audience into an all-enveloping theatrical experience.

This year marks the bicentenary of Paine's death and Griffiths' *A New World: A Life of Thomas Paine* has for that reason alone a current relevance. But it has a more profound contemporary resonance because of the themes it addresses. Paine was writing about a society characterised by widening social inequalities. A wealthy oligarchy of City magnates and landed aristocrats had entrenched itself in Britain as the first British Empire reached its height with the defeat of France in the Seven Years War. In France the aristocracy seized the opportunity presented by the weakness of royal power to strengthen their own position and extend their control over the peasantry. These were the class forces against which Paine contended with his writings. Paine himself appears in Griffiths' play as an unassuming working man. There is none of the self-conscious theatricality of Danton about him. But Paine's writings, of which some powerful sections are voiced during the play, represent his inner core, the essence of Paine's being as a revolutionary. They have an enduring relevance and, in presenting them as he does, Griffiths has demonstrated a tenacity to his principles in a period of political reaction that is worthy of Paine himself.

In years to come those who have seen Griffiths' *A New World: A Life of Thomas Paine* will remember it as an event that had significance far beyond the confines of the theatre. Historians may note it as one of the indications that, as the effects of the recession still reverberated across the river in the City of London, the meaning of revolution was being seriously discussed once more. This is a courageous and far-sighted piece of theatre that connects to the events and concerns of our own time as well as it evokes the history of revolutionary struggles in the eighteenth century.

*   *   *

Songs from
A New World: A Life of Thomas Paine
Shakespeare's Globe Theatre, 2009

Lyrics by Trevor Griffiths
Original music by Stephen Warbeck

The Ballad of Thomas Paine

So it's off with the old and it's on with the new
And it's up with the many and down with the few
It's goodbye to the lion, it's hello to the dove
For we're sailing to the city of brotherly love
Philadelphia's the place, '74's the year,
Thomas Paine's is the story and yours is the ear …

They carried him off on a stretcher of flax
And they pushed him away in a cart
And the lass paid his diggings the while he was ill
For he'd won his way into her heart
Ma Downey's the place, winter the season,
Paine on his back in a struggle for reason …

Whores, sailors and deckmen, rogues, pimps, and drunks
Defrocked lawyers and derelicts all stinking like skunks
Find refuge in Race Street at the bottom of the pit
And drink themselves daft as they sink in the shit.
Race Street's the place, '75's the year,
Common Sense is the issue, the crisis is near …

So it's off with the new and it's back to the old
One story completed, one more to be told,
To England we journey and trouble ahead
The country in turmoil, the people in dread,
The French up in arms in old Liberty's name
Revolution the flag, the sword and the flame.

Spring Fair's in Town

> Spring Fair's in Town
> May the maypole stand tall
> Let a smile melt your frown
> Turn the world upside down
> Let the lowly grow rich
> And the mighty take a fall
> Here the beggar wears the crown
> Spring Fair's in Town.
> But what we dare not ask for
> Is the very thing we need;
> In the darkness it is waiting
> In the soil is set the seed.
> (Whisper) Independence! Independence!

A Call to Arms

> Come to the call, come to the call
> Come to the call to arms
> Fetch yer musket 'n' fetch your stave
> Fetch yer shot and yer stones
> Six months is all we ask of ye
> Then it's back to yer farms
> And it's back to yer homes
> And it's back to yer dear wives' arms.

Joy to the World (traditional; tune by Handel)

> Joy to the World! The Lord is come
> Let earth receive her king
> Let every heart prepare him room
> And heaven and nature sing
> And heaven and nature sing
> And heaven, and heaven, and nature sing …
>
> He rules the world with truth and grace
> And makes the nations prove
> The glories of his righteousness
> And wonders of his love
> And wonders of his love
> And wonders, wonders, of his love.

The Firecake Song

No meat, no meat,
So what do we eat?
Flour and water
Cooked on hot stone
Then off to the slaughter
Like dogs to a bone
Firecake, no meat,
Flour and water
And no retreat.

Will is Dead

Will is dead.
The world turns.
Trees leaf and bud.
Eggs hatch.
Sun burns
Dry thatch.
Will is dead
For a loaf of bread.

Ça Ira (tune: traditional)

Ah! Ça ira, ça ira, ça ira
Les aristocrates à la lanterne!
Ah! Ça ira, ça ira, ça ira
Les aristocrates on les pendra!

If we don't hang 'em
We'll crush 'em
If we don't crush 'em
We'll burn 'em.

Ah! Ça ira, ça ira, ça ira
Les aristocrates à la lanterne!
Ah! Ça ira, ça ira, ça ira
Les aristocrates on les pendra!

And when we've strung 'em all up
We'll stuff a spade up their arse.

Your eyes are green as valleys

Your eyes are green as valleys
Your hair like corn gone wrong
Your lips like shepherds' warnings
Your voice the turtle's song
O come to me my lovely
And no delays
The road ahead awaits us
And better days.

The Slow Jig of Time

So we'll sing for tomorrow,
If singing's no crime;
And what's lacking we'll borrow
From the slow jig of time.

Sure, the roads may be parting,
Given how the land lies;
No more gentle sweethearting,
No more dance to our eyes;

Still we head for tomorrow,
Still our reason to rhyme;
Where we'll sing without sorrow
To the sweet jig of time.

A Hewer's Dream

I'm a hewer of wood
On another man's land
And why he should own it
I'll never understand

Now a Hewer's no brains
As all wise folk know
But a Hewer can dream
From the dark down below

And I dream'd I was flying
As free as the air
In the sky above England
My country so fair

And below I heard weeping
And screaming and pain
And I look'd for its cause
And saw profit and gain

And further afield
In the cities and towns
I saw fear I saw hunger
I heard terrible sounds

And all across England,
Across Scotland and Wales,
There lay wealth beyond counting
Weighing justice's scales.

And as I dreamed I was flying
Free as the air
In the skies above England
My country so fair

Came a cry slowly lifting
Full of purpose and power
Tho' our blood run in rivers
We will take this no more

And O they join'd in a union
Of bodies and minds
They marched on the future
The past left behind

And the battle was quick
And the battle was fair
But the old world was broken
And a new one was there

*   *   *

Reviews

Conscience

Ozgur Heval Cinar and Coskun Usterci, *Conscientious Objection: Resisting Militarised Society*, Zed Books, 272 pages, hardback ISBN 9781848132771, £75, paperback ISBN 9781848132788, £19.99

This interesting and, at times, mildly irritating book is a very useful contribution to the scholarship of conscientious objection. It consists of twenty-three essays, the majority of which have been written by Turkish authors. Many were presented at a conference on this subject held in January 2007 at Istanbul's Bilgi University. Granted the cultural and legal hostility to conscientious objection in Turkey, it is a surprise that the conference went ahead at all. But then the Turkish Government wants to prove its European credentials. Already a member of the Council of Europe, it wants to be granted membership of the European Union as well. In this area of human rights it has a long way to go to catch up with the rest of Europe. Essay after essay makes this very clear indeed.

There are ways of escaping Turkish conscription, but they are not based on any legal recognition of human rights. Homosexuality is one ground for exemption, but the ways in which sexual orientation has to be proved are disgusting beyond belief.

The book is not only concerned with the situation in Turkey. There are contributions covering Greece, Spain, Chile, South Africa and other countries. The description of what went on, in the past, in Spain rang a few bells with me. I well remember being told, by an official at the Spanish Embassy in London, that 'to be a Spaniard and a catholic is to be a soldier'.

This was their response to our Pax Christi opposition to the cat and mouse game played by the Franco Government with the lives of young men refusing to fight in the colonial African wars. As in many other countries, it was the Jehovah's Witnesses who led the way and who suffered greatly in regimes on both sides of the communist/capitalist divide.

An interesting book, but why is it irritating? Because there seems to be an underlying conviction expressed by many that objectors who are not inspired by a collective desire to reform society, but who base their decisions on personal and moral grounds, are somehow second class citizens in the world of conscientious objection. The real CO needs to be 'anti-patriarchal, anti-heteronormative, anti-homophobic and pro-feminist', one author suggests. Some of my heroes amongst those who have refused at great cost, such as Franz Jagerstatter who was executed in August '43, had no notion of social change at all. But they stood and died for a moral principle.

It is also a little irritating that the reader is meant to have more than working knowledge of European legal and political structures. Without such knowledge it is difficult to follow the ramifications of the legal road to the recognition of conscientious objection as a human right.

The 'historical' essays were of great interest to me. I had no idea how much influence Prussian militarism had on the Turkish state long before Attaturk arrived on the scene. Universal conscription we owe of course to Napoleon, but it was refined and polished by Kaiser Wilhelm 1, who launched the phrase about 'the nation in arms'.

The Prussians set about the wholesale militarisation of the state. Said a German-trained Turkish Staff major, in 1908, 'there is no separation between the army and the nation'.

'Peace time should be regarded as the continuation of wartime without fighting,' said another. Militarised as our own British society is today, we have little idea of how the army still dominates in Turkish life, which is why granting rights to conscientious objectors is so difficult.

The global statistics are of great interest too. There are at the moment 192 'sovereign' states. More than 20 have no armed forces. 168 of them do and 80 of those rely on volunteer forces. Some 88 still depend on conscription. Turkey is the only member of the Council of Europe not to grant alternative service rights to COs. There are devious ways of escaping service in Turkey, so it is probably only the most honest and straightforward who find themselves in head-on collision with the law.

What the book does not deal with is how we can resist the claims of a militarised society even if we are not confronted with the call to arms. Supporting 'Conscience', once known as the Peace Tax Campaign, is one such way. Choice of occupation is another. I have always felt that when Joseph Rotblat refused to continue to work on the atomic bomb, in 1944, that his was a CO stance.

Not everything can go into 272 pages. There is more than enough in this book to make it both important and useful.

Bruce Kent

Nemesis

George Monbiot, *Heat: How to Stop the Planet from Burning*, 336 pages, South End Press, updated 2009, paperback ISBN 9780896087873, $18
David Strahan, *The Last Oil Shock: A survival guide to the imminent extinction of petroleum man*, 304 pages, John Murray, paperback ISBN 9780719564246, £8.99
Tristram Stuart, *Waste: Uncovering the Global Food Scandal*, 496 pages, Penguin, ISBN 978-0141036342, £9.99
Jeremy Leggett, *Half Gone: Oil, Gas, , Hot Air and the Global Energy Crisis*, Portobello Books, 322 pages, paperback ISBN 9781846270055, £8.99

Nemesis is the fate that awaits humans' overweening pride. The human species is the only animal which fouls its own nest, which wastes most of the food it collects, and which uses more resources than it creates. And it is the only animal which is conscious of its actions. It knows what it is doing, but still does it, however harmful to itself. Humans have survived and multiplied by dominating their environment, but this way leads to disaster. For long we were in denial. Marion King Hubbert's prediction of the oil peak was first published in 1956, Rachel Carson's 'Silent Spring' appeared in 1962, the Club of Rome warned of *The Limits to Growth* in the 1970s, and Peter Peeters added, in 1979, warnings of wars for resources by the year 2010. A host of books has been published in the last few years, of which the four under review here are among the latest. The warnings are becoming insistent, but they may be too late, unless actions are taken by governments and individuals NOW. These books tell us what we could still do to stave off disaster.

It has become obvious to everyone that the climate is changing, but doubts remain about the seriousness of the effects on human lives. No one who reads the latest paperback edition of George Monbiot's book, *Heat,* can still have any doubts. Glaciers really are shrinking and ice floes melting as the temperature of the sea rises, low lying lands are being flooded and hurricanes increasing. And this is due to human activity, involving the release of what are called 'greenhouse' gases – carbon dioxide and methane – through production and consumption of fuel mainly for heat and power and transport, through the destruction of forests, which absorb these carbons, and through waste in the production and disposal of food. Thus it is that all three of the issues raised in the three books under review are connected – the heating up of the planet's surface, the oil shock, and our food waste. As supplies of oil run out, alternative sources of energy will have to emit no more greenhouse gases than oil, and one way to reduce total emissions would be to tackle food waste.

The central fact which we are being asked to recognise is that economic growth, as we have known it, is not sustainable. Something has to go. We have relied on steadily increasing supplies of energy being available for more production and consumption. Economists, as David Strahan points out, have always neglected, or at least underplayed, the element of energy in economic growth. Sources of energy have been literally undervalued, extra energy being assumed to contribute about 5% to generate growth, when 70% would be nearer the truth. Most of this energy comes from oil. Those scientists who have investigated the oil deposits in the planet's surface believe that they have by now all been discovered, although not all proven. With this knowledge they calculate that about half of this total has already been used up, and oil production will peak within a few years. Maintaining current rates of consumption, which are increasing every year, must therefore be from a steadily declining pool. The result will inevitably be escalating prices and sudden disruptions when particular sources run out.

Some optimists believe that the large deposits of tar sands in Canada and elsewhere can still be developed, but Strahan quotes experts who warn that this development requires the use of water and gas; and gas reserves are subject to the same limits as oil. Others have been putting their faith in bio-fuels produced from agricultural crops. The development of bio-fuels has already put up the price of cereals, to the great disadvantage of those poor families whose very lives depend on the availability of cheap food. Agricultural products are now being used in place of petro-chemicals in the manufacture of plastics. We are also eating more meat, which needs much more input of grains than a vegetarian diet. So, our food supplies are under pressure from three directions. The result is the further destruction of forests to make land available for the production of grains, and this only adds to the gases in the atmosphere and accelerates global warming.

So, what can be done? All governments are promising to make reductions in the greenhouse gas emissions from their countries. The aim is to prevent a global warming greater than 2 degrees centigrade by making continuous reductions up to the year 2030. For the UK this would mean a cut of 91% in emissions per head. Most British Government figures, according to Monbiot, only include carbon dioxide emissions, and another fifth should be added for other gases such as methane. Worse than this, their target would imply, according to the Government's Stern Report, a rise of 3 degrees centigrade of warming. Rather surprisingly, Monbiot quotes a Conservative

Party statement that would seek to stabilise Co2 concentrations at a level below the 2 degrees centigrade equivalent. This would imply draconian restrictions on air and car travel, a massive increase in renewable sources of energy, from wind turbines, photo-voltaic solar panels, ground source heat pumps, and the conversion of electricity generation to combined heat and power production in small-scale gas-fired power stations.

Carbon trading has got a bad name because it has seemed to be a way for the rich, who are most responsible for emissions, to buy rights to be allowed to make these by paying the poor who make the least. But what are called *tradable energy quotas* are put forward in Strahan's book as the best way of persuading individuals, businesses and governments to accept the limitations that have to be made to control global warming. Each country would have a carbon budget for each year set by an independent energy policy committee, like the Bank of England's interest rate committee. The budget would be shared out in rations of so many units for individuals, government and businesses. These could be assessed like taxation and would make everyone think seriously about their carbon footprint. Then ration holders could buy or sell units, according to their needs, but with a cap to prevent hogging.

The big issue would be the size of the initial national budgets, which would have to be agreed internationally, and would have to penalise the big polluters. Would they ever agree to make savings? Some could perhaps be shamed by exposure of the facts. One great advantage of such a scheme would be that individuals, governments and businesses would be encouraged to work out ways of co-operating, for example, by reducing trade, car sharing, combining deliveries, saving waste, and so on. Waste of food is a very largely unrecognised cause of the unnecessary use of energy and gas emissions.

Tristram Stuart's book provides a shocking revelation of a crying scandal in our wasteful food habits. Between the food grower and the consumer something like a half of what is produced goes to waste. The supermarkets are the main culprits, in their practices of overstocking, transporting food long distances, homogenising everything, so that potatoes, tomatoes, carrots and bananas, for example, have to have no irregularities, and rejecting the rest. But farmers themselves waste great quantities of produce and land by all increasing production when prices rise. Most consumers, moreover, throw away all their parings, peel and banana skins, tea and coffee grounds, and made up foods that have passed their 'sell by' date. All these could go to pig swill.

Jeremy Leggett was a lecturer in Earth Sciences at Imperial College, then an oil company consultant, but became, in 1989, UK chief scientist for Greenpeace and is now chief executive of Solarcentury, the UK's largest independent solar electric company. As such he has credibility when he writes regularly for *The Guardian,* and warned as recently as September 3rd this year, that 'Peak Oil' can only be a few years away even after the new oil discoveries in the Gulf of Mexico and elsewhere. 'Peak Oil' is the term used by the oil experts for the time when oil consumption begins to exceed oil availability from current production and proven available reserves. Oil prices are already around five times what they were in the 1960s, and can be expected to rise even faster as supplies are depleted. The same applies to natural gas. Leggett's *Half Gone* argues the case for early topping of the peak, but combines this with dire warnings of the effect on the planet's climate of oil consumption at current, ever growing rates.

Leggett is at pains to explain how it came about that the oil experts have been for so long in denial. The giant oil companies obviously wished to maintain their dominant position in the world economy, but to this end exaggerated the size of reserves they held. Governments were heavily influenced by the oil companies, but also tended to think no further into the future than the next election. Only the few independent experts such as Leggett at Greenpeace did that, and the general public, enjoying the pleasures of high consumption, had no desire to listen to the warnings of a bunch of 'Green' fanatics. Only very recently opinion has begun to change as oil prices rise and climate shows every sign of change. But what to do about the increasing carbon footprint is quite unclear. Small savings in electricity used is about as far as popular opinion has reached, and a certain sense that the credit crunch and rising unemployment may be a blessing in disguise (for some).

Leggett's book has changed and reinforced my own thinking. This has been changed in relation to the timing of the 'peak', which I now accept must come very soon indeed, and reinforced it in relation to the alternatives available to reduce our ever-rising oil consumption. Leggett shows how the oil companies really have exaggerated their existing production capacities and their oil reserves, and the potential use of tar sand deposits. The latter would themselves require enormous quantities of oil and also of water to develop. Of the non-carbon creating alternatives, coal liquefaction and sequestration are ruled out on the grounds of cost compared with the use of energy from sun, wind and waves. Nuclear power is ruled out for the same reason, but also because of the problems of disposing of the nuclear waste and preventing terrorist sabotage.

Why, then, are we not pressing governments by every means at our disposal to step up work – which would give jobs to those unemployed as a result of the financial crisis – on developing the alternative energy sources from the sun, the wind and the waves? The explanation is that this would involve a revolution, not necessarily a political revolution, but a revolution in our thinking. Instead of relying on giant plants, vast refineries, national grids and innumerable distribution networks, the alternatives would mean local, individual and community action. The example is given by Leggett of the small town of Woking in Surrey, which since 1990 has cut its carbon dioxide emissions by three quarters, using a hybrid energy system, involving private wires, CHP — Combined Heat and Power — in groups of buildings (mostly natural gas but some bio-mass), solar PV – Photo Voltaic cells – and energy efficiency, plus some fuel cells and absorption chillers . Old peoples' homes and housing estates had made their own mini-energy worlds. The grid could go for ever. My only doubt is about bio-mass if this means competition with food supplies. But what matters is that a whole community would have to act together. If a town of 80,000 could do it, Ken Livingstone employed the Woking energy manager (Allan Jones) to do it for London's 8 million. What is Boris Johnson doing?

None of this suggests that we can avoid a total reduction in our energy use – in cars, air flights, heating, freezing, lighting, air conditioning – through more and better public transport, car pooling, holidays at home, house insulation, nil waste, communal services. All this once again implies a revolution in our attitude to consumption both as individuals and communities. Leggett is optimistic, believing that a beginning has already begun and change will accelerate as new habits develop, and the example of Woking is copied and we see in Sweden the Government, local and national, business, academics, and farmers reach their aim of becoming an oil-free economy in a decade. It can be done.

Each of these books contains long lists of what we could all begin to do to reduce the dangers of climate change. But governments have to do far more – not only taxing the big spenders, but subsidising and developing non-fossil forms of energy and, above all, coming clean about the real facts of oil depletion, climate change and waste, and educating the public in the implications of these facts.

Michael Barratt Brown
who three decades ago installed solar panels on the
roof of his Derbyshire home, and recently installed new ones.

Radiation and Consent

Ellen Leopold, *Under the Radar – Cancer and the Cold War,* **Rutgers University Press, 304 pages, hardback ISBN 9780813544045, £23.50**

Ellen Leopold is described in Google searches as an independent researcher and as a member of the Women's Community Cancer Project in Cambridge, Massachusetts. Her first book on cancer, *A Darker Ribbon: Women and their Doctors in the Twentieth Century, A Social History of Breast Cancer,* was published in 1999. Like Rachel Carson, author of *Silent Spring,* she is herself a breast cancer survivor.

Ionising radiation and consent are the connections that Ellen Leopold makes between cancer and the Cold War, and she establishes them firmly in the early pages of this book. She refers to the *Down-winders* of Nevada and the estimated 140,000 fatal cancers caused by atmospheric testing of nuclear weapons in the United States. At the end of the Cold War, in 1999, Karl Z Morgan, an Atomic Energy Commission physicist, stated that

> 'The greatest irony of our atmospheric nuclear testing program is that the only victims of US nuclear weapons since World War II have been our own people.'

No one is on record as having sought the consent of the Down-winders.

Leopold begins her book with an account of the similar hubris in the use of cobalt radiation therapy for breast cancer in the 1950s, which injured, among others, Irma Nathanson, a young mother in Wichita, Kansas. The detail is available in the record of *Nathanson v Kline,* which Leopold uses to create a carefully detailed but highly readable and gripping account of the arguments for informed consent. Nathanson sued her radiologist, John R Kline, after years of painful medical treatments for the injuries caused by what are now regarded as exceptional doses of cobalt 60 radiation, advised by Kline as a precaution against a recurrence of cancer after apparently successful mastectomy. The radiation wounds to her chest were such that successive attempts to close the chest cavity by skin grafting failed. She was transferred to the care of a surgeon who was specialised in the treatment of radiation injuries suffered by workers at Eniwetok Atoll after nuclear weapon tests in the late 1940s.

Dead tissue, muscle, cartilage and several ribs had to be removed before further skin grafts could be attempted. Irma Nathanson had already lost the use of her left arm, which later became gangrenous, requiring amputation of the lower part, and her left lung was collapsed. The court case ended with an out-of-court settlement of an undisclosed sum for the plaintiff with costs against the radiologist and the hospital. The case is significant for the plaintiff's evidence of a lack of informed consent. No evidence of her being advised of the possible consequences of cobalt 60 radiation treatment was offered, and Justice Schroeder's opinion on the nature and limitations of informed consent has influenced later litigation and medical practice. Surprisingly, the disabled Irma Nathanson survived for another 33 years until she died of other, possibly related, cancers.

The author makes a penetrating analysis of the effect of the Cold War on the American public. Here is a sample of her writing.

'When the anti-Soviet propaganda became less shrill and air raid drills less frequent, the sense of imminent danger began to fade. Further disarmament treaties with the Soviet Union in 1974 and 1978 enhanced the growing sense of national security. With it came a relaxation of the command structures that had held traditional social hierarchies in place and unaware of one another.

The loosening of the doctor-patient relationship owes something to this easing of the prevailing crisis mentality just as it does to the rise in feminine consciousness. As one grew weaker the other grew stronger. The feeling of stepping back from the brink permitted Americans to speak more openly, to pursue pent-up grievances closer to home without the fear of reprisals. Authority in any guise (whether professional, corporate, elected, or male) could now be challenged with greater impunity. Many activist groups were set to try.'

One of the effects of the Cold War secrecy described by the author is that only one person in five in the USA thought that fall-out was dangerous, even though half a million people had been exposed to it without their agreement, and many of them died as a result. The author records that it had been seen as unpatriotic to question the bomb tests. Interestingly, she notes that the nuclear industry found in its surveys that women 'lack nuclear enthusiasm'. The explanation could be that women have good reason to fear the mutagenic effects of radiation and other agents on the foetus and the possibility of giving birth to a seriously deformed child.

The author's analysis extends to an examination of the nuclear regulators, the pressures for deregulation by those constrained by regulation, the structure of the International Commission on Radiological Protection (ICRP), the accountability of the World Health Organisation to the International Atomic Energy Agency on radiation matters, and the application of the precautionary principle.

The author has other useful insights into the pharmaceutical industry's search for anti-cancer drugs and the lack of meaningful surveys into the overall long-term effects of the 'war on cancer'. She leaves open the question of why cancer mortality has doubled in the USA since World War

Two (but she mentions the relative success in the control of cardio-vascular disease), and she speculates on the development of a culture in which cancer patients, and not only those who use tobacco and alcohol, can be made to feel responsible for their ill health. She questions the American Medical Association's sometimes unquestioning acceptance of the uses of radiation in diagnosis and treatment without adequate audit of each patient's cumulative exposure, and she sees a need for better public understanding of the way in which radiation is measured. She notes that people know more about risk measurement in diet than they do about radiation. The considerable benefits of the CT (computerised tomography) scanning, for example, have to be set against a dose exceptionally as high as 44 millisieverts for a pelvic area scan – double the annual dose allowed to a worker in the nuclear industry, and 44 times higher than a nuclear industry dose to a member of the public.

We need more authors with the capable and penetrating curiosity of Ellen Leopold, Helen Caldicott, author of *Nuclear Power is Not the Answer* (reviewed in Spokesman 99), and Rosalie Bertell who wrote 'Why Chernobyl Still Matters' for the *Journal of Humanitarian Medicine* (reproduced in 2003 in *Spokesman 78*) in which she, too, detailed the structural inadequacies of the UN nuclear agencies and the 'self-established' International Commission on Radiological Protection. That authors on nuclear matters be independent of the industry is becoming even more necessary as commercial confidentiality is added to government secrecy and misinformation.

Christopher Gifford

Victor's Justice

John Laughland, *A History of Political Trials: From Charles I to Saddam Hussein*, Peter Lang, 316 pages, paperback ISBN 9781906165000, £12.99

This is a meticulously documented study of the trials or former heads or state: Charles I and Louis XVI; the leaders of the French Third Republic; Marshal Petain, Quisling, the Nazi and Japanese leaders; war-time leaders in Czechoslovakia, Hungary, Bulgaria, Finland and Greece; the Greek colonels, Emperor Bokassa and the Argentine generals; more recently, Ceaucescu, Honecker, Kambanda in Rwanda, Milosevic and Saddam Hussein. The book uses history admirably to illuminate current issues. It refutes the widespread assertion that the trial of former political leaders, which is becoming increasingly common, is unprecedented, and argues convincingly that the trials conducted by the special tribunals for Yugoslavia and Rwanda, and the International Criminal Court, have much in common with earlier political trials.

There have been no acquitals of heads of state. As Danton said, 'A king is dead as soon as he appears in front of his judges'. The trials of both kings were political and even religious acts, calculated to find a scapegoat and consolidate the new regime.

Laughland draws attention to the irregularities which have characterised all the trials, not to exonerate the defendants, at least morally, but to show that, in all such trials, the prosecution is as political as the defence, and to look at the profound *constitutional* issues raised by the trials.

In the nineteenth century, international laws to regulate war were formulated at the Hague and Geneva. The enemy was considered to have the right to fight, and from this flowed the provisions for the humane treatment of prisoners. The First World War saw a return to a Manichean view of the enemy as the embodiment of evil. The Treaty of Versailles asserted Germany's exclusive war guilt and called for the trial of the Kaiser. It applied retrospective rules, prosecuted individuals on the losing side rather than laying down a general law, and proclaimed the defendants guilty in advance. Subsequent trials, including those by the special tribunals for Yugoslavia and Rwanda, have also been 'victor's justice' and done the same. They have also rejected 'legal formalities' concerning evidence; used anonymous witnesses and 'expert witnesses' who have witnessed nothing; suppressed evidence and falsified trial reports; and introduced 'joint criminal conspiracy' by which a defendant can be convicted of a crime which he did not commit, order, know about or intend. In the Rwandan case – the defining event in subsequent military interventions and trials – the former Prime Minister was found guilty of genocide without a trial, on the basis of a confession which he immediately withdrew, claiming that it was made under duress, for fear of his family's safety, and following advice by a lawyer imposed on him by the prosecution, who was a friend of the prosecutor.

Laughland questions whether acts of state can be treated like private crimes. His criticism of the 'new' system of international law is not only that it perverts justice and history and rarely encourages reconciliation, but also that it has undermined the old one. It is linked with a 'liberal imperialist' project which rejects the constraints of 'classical' international law, in pursuit of which the United States and the Nato countries have undertaken aggressive war, state destruction, 'coercive' bombing, mass population expulsions, and the torture of prisoners.

The question remains, what should be done when oppressive regimes are overthrown? Laughland does not answer this question because it is a political judgement to which no simple answer can be laid down in advance.

A good regime trial would be one in which the new sovereign displayed the political virtues as Aristotle defined them; courage, moderation, magnanimity and prudence. Today's human rights advocates, by contrast, are inspired by a punishment ethic which sits ill with these virtues, and which often prefers war over peace in the name of 'justice'.

Laughland points out that war crimes are already covered by the Geneva and Hague Conventions. Such crimes can and should be prosecuted under these Conventions, but national tribunals are preferable to international ones because they are more deeply embedded in the national culture and more open to the checks and balances of public opinion. The programme to create new international tribunals and a new jurisdiction is a similar blunt instrument to the punishment of tyrannical kings by revolutionary republican tribunals in the past.

It is hard to read this book without concluding that the trials organised by the special tribunals and the International Criminal Court have been a perversion of the judicial process, and a backward step in the development of international humanitarian law. It is impossible, in a short review, to convey the scope, depth, and incisiveness of this iconoclastic book. I can only urge people concerned with the rule of law to read it.

Graham Hallett

Graham Hallett is the author of European Security in the Post-Soviet Age: The Case against Nato *(www.caseagainstnato.co.uk).*

Slaves

Cynthia Mc Leod, *The Free Negress Elisabeth*, translated from the Dutch by Brian Doyle, Arcadia Books, 320 pages, paperback ISBN 9781905147830, £11.99

'Rothschild and Freshfields founders had links to slavery, papers reveal'. That was the lengthy, front-page headline of the *Financial Times* on 28 June 2009, above its photograph of a nineteenth century ledger of 'Slave Compensation Counter Claims' for the Colony of St Christopher, now known as St Kitt's, in the West Indies.

Freshfields is one of the City's 'top four "Magic Circle" UK law firms', according to the FT. One of its founders, James William Freshfield, 'counterclaimed' for three groups of slaves in St Christopher, basing the claim on unpaid legal fees regarding an earlier sale of the Belle Tête estate and its slaves. The claim, which was later withdrawn, was made under a Government compensation scheme for slave owners, following the partial abolition of slavery in the 1830s.

Nathan Mayer Rothschild and his brother, Baron James de Rothschild, agreed that £3,000 owed to Lord James O'Bryen by the purchaser of his estate in Antigua should be secured to NM Rothschild himself by a mortgage over 88 slaves on the estate. The slaves were collateral in case the debtor defaulted, which he duly did. NM Rothschild used the compensation scheme to secure the £3,000, which was eventually awarded to his estate after his death.

These revelations follow discoveries made in the National Archives at Kew, which have been prominently reported in the FT. They could be costly, both financially and in turns of reputation, for modern-day and high profile descendents of those whose wealth was bolstered by the proceeds of the slave trade. During three centuries, that trade shipped some eleven million people across the Atlantic Ocean from Africa to the Americas and West Indies. Some of their descendants are acutely aware of a need for redress.

The story of *The Free Negress Elizabeth* Samson pre-dates the events reported in the FT. Her diaries recount her experiences in the Dutch colony of Suriname in South America during the eighteenth century, as well as in Holland itself, where she travelled to clear her name of a trumped-up legal charge. Elisabeth's mother had her freedom purchased before her daughter was born. Elisabeth was therefore never a slave herself, hence the description 'Free'. In addition, she was gifted in music and business, activities which were encouraged in the household where she grew up. She steadily accumulated considerable personal wealth, much to the envy of other plantation owners in Suriname, who were growing coffee and sugar for the Dutch market, using slave labour. Her long-term partner and the man she wished to marry, Carl Otto Creutz, pre-deceased her.

Marriage between blacks and whites was actively discouraged in eighteenth century Suriname, if not expressly banned, as many colonists maintained. Elisabeth contested this alleged ban when she married Hermanus Daniel Zobre, following Creutz's death. She was to die herself only a few years later, leaving most of her property to her young husband, and thus to the white community, as the colony's administrators had hoped.

Abolition of slavery was still many decades away, yet opposition amongst escaped slaves, known as Maroons, was becoming steadily bolder. The Maroons, as well as the slaves themselves, had much to fear from the colonists. Physical punishment was frequent and brutal. Execution was summary for Maroons who were caught. Yet the interactions of colonists and slaves were intimate and fecund. Many mixed-race children, described as mulattos, were born. But Elisabeth herself never had children. This didn't excuse her from denunciations from the pulpit of the Dutch church she attended, and supported financially, in Paramaribo, the capital of Suriname.

Cynthia Mc Leod is the daughter of the last governor and first president of Suriname. She has written a restrained account of Elisabeth's experiences, elegantly translated by Brian Doyle, and equipped with a useful glossary. It is, at the same time, something of a chronicle of the vicissitudes of the Dutch Empire during the eighteenth century. But, most of all, it is testimony to slavery's financial enrichment of Europe, and Elisabeth's self-emancipation.

Tony Simpson

Scots in Spain

Daniel Gray, *Homage to Caledonia: Scotland and the Spanish Civil War*, Luath Press, 256 pages, paperback ISBN13 9781906817169, £9.99

Each year in Glasgow a group of labour movement activists gather on the banks of the Clyde in front of Customs House, at the other side of the suspension bridge from where Glasgow Trades Council used to meet. They gather at the base of the statue of Dolores Ibárruri – La Pasionaria. They gather in memory of the contribution of the Scottish volunteers to Republican Spain, to fight the Falangist fascists in the Spanish Civil War.

The Spanish Civil War was a call to arms for 2,300 British volunteers, of which more than 500 were from Scotland. The first book of its kind, Daniel Gray's *Homage to Caledonia* examines Scotland's role in the conflict, detailing exactly why Scottish involvement was so profound. The book moves chronologically through events and places, firstly surveying the landscape in contemporary Scotland before describing volunteers' journeys to Spain, and then tracing their every involvement from arrival to homecoming (or not). There is also an account of the non-combative role, from fundraising for Spain and medical aid, to political manoeuvrings within the volatile Scottish Left.

It may come as a surprise, but the legacy of divisions over this issue on the Left in Scotland can resurface even today. I can remember being at a screening of Ken Loach's film *Land and Freedom* in Dundee when it reached the scenes following the falling-out between the communists and the POUM (Workers' Party of Marxist Unification). At this point two elderly comrades in front of me became particularly agitated, and started providing the audience with an alternative narrative, only to be confronted by another elderly voice from within the darkness of the cinema declaring he had been there and Loach was right.

Using a wealth of previously unpublished letters sent back from the front as well as other archival items, Daniel Gray is able to tell little known stories of courage in conflict, and to call into question accepted versions of events such as the murder of Bob Smillie, or the heroism of 'The Scots Scarlet Pimpernel'.

Homage to Caledonia offers a very human take on events in Spain. For every tale of abject distress in a time of war, there is a tale of a Scottish volunteer urinating in his general's boots, knocking back a dram with Errol Flynn, or appalling Spanish comrades with his pipe playing.

What does come through from *Homage to Caledonia* is the level of political awareness amongst the volunteers, which was added to, no doubt, by the provision of political education within the battalions. They recognised that, under the circumstances of advancing fascism, not to intervene is to intervene, especially when the fascists are being supported externally. The Brigaders, or particularly the ILP element from Scotland, had sussed out that the republicans' decision not to include a social revolution within their struggle was a mistake, which would weaken their political appeal to the masses. There was no doubt as to what Franco's objectives were. The foresight shown in these arguments from the Left can be found in what followed, in that it took until the 1980s before Spain, Portugal and Greece managed to leave behind NATO supported totalitarian rule for good and become members of the European Union

At the beginning of his book, Daniel Gray quotes from another on the subject, *From the Calton to Catalonia* by John and Willy Maley (Glasgow City Libraries). The extract is written in Glaswegian Scots and describes conditions in the East End of Glasgow in the 1930s.

> 'When they three (Franco, Mussolini, Hitler) goat thegither an came up against the Spanish workers, they didnae expect the Calton tae offer handers.'

This extract encapsulates the poverty from which many of the proportionately large number of Scots volunteers who went to Spain came. It also emphasises their vision.

> 'They wur internationalists. They wur Europeans. They wur Scots.'

Gray's book, acknowledged in its Foreword by Tony Benn as 'important and powerful', is not only a culmination of extensive academic research, but also a personal gathering of information from relatives of International Brigaders and the now sadly deceased Steve Fullarton, the last Scottish

International Brigader.

Daniel Gray includes a chronology of events showing clear links from the General Strike of 1926 through to the Spanish Civil War itself, to Franco's victory in 1939, Hitler's invasion of Poland, and the start of World War Two.

Gray's writing style is easy to read and the text is accompanied by photographs throughout. Although in his introduction he says the book is 'a social history rather than a military one', he does of necessity speak of events experienced by the Brigaders in relation to the war and turbulent politics of the time. He makes it clear that the period should be viewed 'through the prism of 1930s Scotland', a time of hope and high ideals that may seem foreign in our more cynical, individualistic times. The overwhelming sentiments that come across in the book from the Brigaders and, indeed, from their families are those of pride in having taken part, and their lack of regret in doing so. It is inspiring and humbling in equal measure.

It is seventy years since Glasgow welcomed home from foreign fields a group of its soldier sons. They had not, though, volunteered for service in the regular army, but as members of the International Brigades that participated on the republican side in the Spanish Civil War. *The Glasgow Herald* marked the Brigaders' 11th December 1938 return from Spain with a fascinating account of their arrival. A vast crowd gathered at Central Station to greet the men, many of them waiting, as the *Herald* reported, 'to hear whether their relatives and friends who had gone out to Spain were returning or had been killed in action'.

The stories of many of the 90 volunteers who returned to Glasgow that day, and the other 500 Scots who participated in Spain, are contained in *Homage to Caledonia: Scotland and the Spanish Civil War*, which is the first book to document and celebrate the great sacrifices made by Scots and Scotland for the Spanish republic. It demonstrates the extent to which Glasgow and Scotland turned the Spanish war into their own.

Henry McCubbin

Mayakovsky

Vladimir Mayakovsky, *Pro Eto – That's What*, translated by Larisa Gureyeva and George Hyde, illustrated by Alexander Rodchenko, Arc Publications, 172 pages, paperback ISBN 9781904614319, £12.99

Mayakovsky's is one of the more recognisable faces of the Russian Revolution. While Lenin bestrode the platform, leaning forward to emphasise his points to the crowd, all captured on movie film, in this volume Mayakovsky is deceptively still and solid, darkened eyes beneath a heavy brow and woollen cap. He inhabits Rodchenko's playful photomontages which interpret, rather literally, the tortured progress of the poet's own 'Ballad of Reading Gaol', proceeding to 'Christmas Eve', and culminating in a concluding section revealingly entitled 'Application on Behalf of ... please, comrade chemist, fill it in yourself'.

The rhythm seems to echo Oscar Wilde's own relentless rumble, which is captured very well in this feisty translation:

> The music of the ballad sure ain't new –
> but if its words are words of pain
> and its words describe the pain again
> the ballad too renews its old refrain.

Lily Brik, wife of Mayakovsky's publisher, Osip Brik, was, it seems, the most immediate cause of the poet's pain. *That's What*, a loose translation of the Russian 'Pro Eto', literally 'about this', is 'dedicated to her and to me'. Lily also inhabits Rodchenko's montages, so he seemed to know what Mayakovsky's theme really was, even if the poet was more suggestive and less explicit.

Arc have produced a handsome Russian-English edition of this personal epic of the early years of the Revolution, first published in the LEF journal (Left Front of the Arts) in 1923. George Hyde adds a lively note on 'Translating Mayakovsky's *That's What*'. His co-translator, Larisa Gureyeva, is the granddaughter of V.M. Molotov-Skryabin, co-signatory of the notorious pact with Germany of 1939.

Hyde writes of the 'permissive' 1920s in the early Soviet Union. Following the recent splendid exhibition of Rodchenko and Popova at the Tate Modern (see Spokesman 105), there are increasing signs of a growing interest in the early, tumultuous years of the Russian Revolution.

TS